God and
the Grotesque

God
and the
Grotesque

by Carl Skrade

The Westminster Press
Philadelphia

Scripture quotations from the Revised Standard
Version of the Bible are copyright, 1946 and
1952, by the Division of Christian Education
of the National Council of Churches,
and are used by permission.

Published by The Westminster Press ®
Philadelphia, Pennsylvania

Printed in the United States of America

Acknowledgment is made to the following:

Farrar, Straus & Giroux, Inc., for quotations from *Wise Blood,* by
Flannery O'Connor, copyright © 1949, 1952, 1962 by Flannery
O'Connor; and from "Revelation" from *Everything That Rises
Must Converge,* by Flannery O'Connor, copyright © 1964, 1965 by
the Estate of Mary Flannery O'Connor.

Harcourt Brace Jovanovich, Inc., for quotations from *A Good Man
Is Hard to Find and Other Stories,* copyright © 1953, 1954, 1955
by Flannery O'Connor.

The above quotations from Flannery O'Connor's works are used
by permission of A. M. Heath & Company Ltd. and the Estate of
the late Flannery O'Connor.

Charles Scribner's Sons, for an excerpt from "A Clean, Well-
lighted Place," by Ernest Hemingway in *The Hemingway Reader,*
1953.

The Viking Press, Inc., for quotations from *Three Screenplays:
Viridiana, The Exterminating Angel, Simon of the Desert,* by Luis
Buñuel. Translation © 1969, Grossman Publishers, Inc. Reprinted
by permission of Grossman Publishers.

Library of Congress Cataloging in Publication Data

Skrade, Carl.
  God and the grotesque.

  Includes bibliographical references.
  1. Hope. 2. Theology—20th century. 3. Rational-
ism. 4. Grotesque. I. Title.
BV4638.S56   201   74–10972
ISBN 0–664–20710–3
ISBN 0–664–24995–7 (pbk.)

Χαρις σοι . . .

Contents

Preface

This book is intended for a much wider audience than the readers of traditional theological writings. It is directed to that increasing and broadening spectrum of people from a wide variety of interests and disciplines who are in quest of sources for the renewal of our humanness beyond the traditional battlelines that our culture has come to assume. It is intended for those who feel that there are ways of being beyond the usual conflicts of left and right, conservative and liberal—and beyond the militant lukewarmness, the meaningless middle of the road which is so prominent in our time. This book addresses that vast audience determined not to capitulate to the flabby obscenities of a Watergate world, nor to the manipulations and strictures of a Walden Two, nor to the nihilism of *La Dolce Vita*. For this audience, this book is not a set of answers but a call for hope and dialogue.

This book includes a criticism of technological, death-oriented society with its rationalistic, confined gods and its rationalistic, controlled man—but primarily it is about hope. This hope rests in the reality, encountered over and again by each of us and expressed powerfully and repeatedly in our arts, that man cannot and need not structure time and life and the cosmos in order to make them behave so as to guarantee a future of his own design. This hope presses in on us from beyond the boundaries of reason and the worship of death. It is a hope rooted in the conviction that the nature of being is grace.

Written out of a theological background, this book also speaks to others interested in theology, but it violates some of the traditional rubrics of that discipline. Thus, in part, it may be seen as a request for a rethinking of the scope and methodology of theology.

I appreciate the custom that allows me at this time to thank those to whom I am indebted for their patience and assistance in this work. Most must go unnamed. However, a special thanks is due to Carol, my wife, and to my sons, Peter and Kris, for bearing with me as I wrote. Finally, I wish to thank the staff of The Westminster Press for suggestions that did much to improve the clarity and readability of this work. The responsibility for the problems in this book remain mine, of course.

C. S.

Columbus, Ohio

Introduction

Si tibi vis omnia subjicere, te subjice rationi, said Seneca. "If you wish to subject all things to yourself, subject yourself to reason." This is a pregnant saying, encapsulating as it does that which has been accepted as the highest and best aspiration of Western culture and, at the same time, summarizing the serpent's side of the Fall. Adam and Eve, like Seneca, subjected themselves to reason, to the knowledge of good and evil. We remember this, but we seem to forget that in so choosing they rejected the tree of life.

This powerful insight of the ancient Yahwist and the similar, equally powerful psychoanalytical suggestion that man in the depths of his instincts has chosen life against death are closely interrelated. In his reasonable quest for the knowledge of how to control life, man becomes the obedient servant of death; this aptly characterizes the story of our race, the story of man's attempts to be alone, in control. This is the story that leaves us now at the crossroads which branches off either into the cataclysmic abyss of the nuclear holocaust, the triumph of death in death; or into the bland murk of *1984*, the triumph of death in life.

Theology has not escaped; rather, the main thrust of God-talk in Western culture also, unfortunately, has been bound within the confines of the rational as theologians have argued interminably, generally with impeccable rationale and logic, over such questions as God's existence, attributes, natures, et cetera. We have been tied to this rationalistic approach in spite of recurrent protests throughout our history. But is it possible for God-talk to be meaningful if it eliminates or represses man's very real experience of the non-rational? And is it not possible that there is health and hope beyond the confines of reason? It is the purpose of this book to examine these questions.

Seneca's statement and the primary direction of our culture presuppose that man, via reason, can rule self and cosmos; this implies either that God is not or that he too is subject to reason. But what, exactly, do I mean by reason? What are the hopes we base on it? And what do I mean by rationalism?

By reason I mean not simply the chemical-electrical reactions of certain brain cells that are involved in the cognitive activity, nor do I mean simply man's faculty for thought. Rather, by reason I mean man's act of submission of truth and reality before the bar of the principles of non-contradiction (it is not possible for something to be and not be at the same time) and necessity (what is is necessarily). Anchored in these principles, Western man has proceeded to abstract and to generalize and to formulate absolutes. Armed with these principles, so long assumed self-evident and beyond question, Western man has moved out to conquer the cosmos, to make himself as God. When he encounters that which does not bow before these inviolable "truths," he declares it untrue or unreal or unfit. He dare not allow such things a place in his reasonable universe of law and order.

By rationalism I mean not only the philosophical movements referred to by that title but also the elevation of reason as defined to the position of dominance in the affairs of men. Rationalism is the deification of reason with its principle of non-contradiction and its necessary truths.

But infringing, impinging on the borders of reason from beyond its limits is the experience of Nothing. Thus, even though we live in a time and culture dominated by the rationalistic approach to reality and though we work within theological traditions short-circuited by their lack of attention to the non-rational, nonetheless there is considerable evidence in this same culture of a powerful, uncontrollable emergence of the non-rational. This is true especially in the artistic accomplishments that express a growing awareness of the limits, the "dead end," of a rationalistic approach to reality and go on to suggest the possibility of health beyond Nothingness, hope beyond reason. In the arts, these expressions are thrust before us particularly by the grotesque which has been so abundant in films and paintings and writings and sculptings of recent decades. I define the grotesque according to the common usage of that term in literary and artistic criticism; i.e., the grotesque is that which deviates from the conventional and the normal, that which is incongruous with that deemed real according to consensual validation.

I suggest that our culture is replete with "fearful and

fascinating" experiences and images of these grotesques
which point non-rationally and irrepressibly beyond
themselves to the still real experience of a holy Nothingness, a reality, indeed an ultimate reality, whose freedom
and force shape our present and may open up our fu-
tures in spite of our rationalistic system building.

A theology that accepts its roots in anthropology, a
theology that is based in the belief that the understanding
of man and his situation contains the clearest and most
accurate reflection of our understanding of God, must
give constant and careful consideration to those phenomena which characterize our time. I will argue that the
grotesque is, manifestly, such a phenomenon and thus
demands theological consideration.

More exactly, what does it mean to speak of theology
rooted in anthropology? Some persons react to this idea
as if it involved an entire rejection of any and every
understanding of revelation, or they believe that this
binds God and God-talk to the whims of man and to the
limits of man-talk. Are these just and "necessary" reactions? Or must one conclude that talk of theology as anthropology is a confession, perhaps necessary, of the
bankruptcy of theology? I believe that both such reactions
are in error.

When I speak of theology rooted in anthropology I
mean that the fundamental matrix out of which there
can come meaningful talk of God, or Being Itself, or Ultimate Reality, is the living human experience of the op-
pressive, unchosen question, "To be or not to be?" Passionate and genuine concern with the question of the
meaning of being, concern with the meaning of being
one's self, within this world, with one's finitude and es-
trangements and hopes, is, I believe, the true realm of

theology. The source for talking of such concerns is the concrete human predicament. Thus theology, to be alive, must be willing to look afresh, constantly, without blinking, into the human situation. This means that all that man is and does—in his struggle with these questions or in his struggle to avoid them—should be the focus of theological scrutiny.

Most important, in order to get by the bombast of what we tell each other so that we might get out from under any really serious concern with these questions, I think that we must always go beyond our creeds and confessions, our declarations and constitutions. As we do so, I feel that it becomes evident that one of the most striking features of our culture is our reverberating emptiness. We are indeed Eliot's straw men; we are indeed Tillich's culture without depth.

But, of course, in our time also there are uncontrived, non-plastic struggles with these questions. They go on all about us, within us, and we are able to avoid them only with the greatest of effort. However, it is my judgment that the theologian in exploring these struggles does well to give attention to two loci in particular. On the one hand, he should look to the 'am ha'aretz, the people of the land, the poor, who have not been able to surround themselves with enough tinsel to avoid the basic issues. Secondly, he should look to the arts, theology's next of kin, for I judge that it is in the arts that one is most likely to find confessions—perhaps subconscious, perhaps more felt than understood—of an age's skirmishes with the meaning of being.

Perhaps more than any other age, our age of Muzak is forced to ask such questions as: What is art? To which art should I look? Which artist's struggles must I con-

sider? But these are old and still unanswered questions. I
think that they are akin to the questions that the man in
the streets of Jerusalem had to ask himself concerning
whether he should follow Jeremiah or Hananiah. There
is no formula whereby we can resolve these issues. Instead of seeking to resolve them, I simply offer an interpretation of the grotesque in contemporary arts and culture, noting its prominence and force.

It may be objected that this understanding of theology
as anthropology makes theology too broad, or it may be
said that many disciplines, not just theology, are concerned with these sources and issues. What does distinguish the theologian? In answering this, I would like to
borrow some categories from a well-known article by Paul
Tillich entitled "Existentialist Aspects of Modern Art." [1]
In his discussion of art, Tillich uses the following categories:

1. Non-religious style, non-religious content; i.e., art
that evokes a new and deeper level of reality in ordinary
objects. For example, Jan Steen's *The World Upside
Down*.

2. Religious style, non-religious content. Without references to the traditional religious symbols and subjects, this art radically asks the question of the meaning
of being and courageously and openly faces the human
predicament out of which these questions come. An example of such art is Picasso's *Guernica*.

3. Non-religious style, religious content. Such art does
use typical religious subjects and symbols but nonetheless the art itself obscures the question of the meaning
of being. I suggest that typical Sunday school art is of this
type.

4. Religious style, religious content. The typical reli-

gious symbols and subjects are used, but in such a way as to raise, probably uncomfortably, the question of the meaning of being. A classic example is Grünewald's Isenheim *Crucifixion*.

I suggest that analogous categories may help to identify the theologian and indicate his situation in our time. Traditionally, the theologian is the one who works in a religious style with religious content; i.e., he thinks, writes, and speaks on religious subjects such as God and sin and salvation in such a way as to raise or attempt to raise and deal with the question of the meaning of being within the confines of this framework.

However, because so much of what passes for religious work in our time involves activities concerned with the traditional subjects but effected in such a way as to obscure for individuals the question of the meaning of being (compare category three in Tillich's discussion), I believe that it has become difficult if not impossible for the theologians of religious style and religious content to communicate effectively with any significant number of people.

Therefore, I believe that the theologian today must live somewhere in between religious style–religious content and non-religious style–religious content. Only thus can he escape the sterile and artificial formulas, and hope to communicate out of and into the concrete human predicament. Thus I believe that his work will unavoidably overlap with the work of many others who would not be interested in thinking of themselves as theologians or their work as religious. But does such overlapping constitute any real problem? Why is differentiation of field so necessary? Given our common cultural refusal to face the questions, isn't such arguing over "job descriptions" superfluous? Doesn't it simply grow out of our interest in categorizing and controlling on our own terms? Isn't it simply another way of avoiding the questions?

Perhaps the distinguishing mark of the theologian is that he believes that the key to the question of the meaning of being lies beyond this world of things and formulas and reasons, beyond what man can manage by and for himself on his own terms, in what other generations have called "God." The contemporary theologian may not be able to articulate a content for that word, but this is not necessarily bad. Perhaps this inability to articulate is a "making real" of the traditional distinction between God and man.

For the sake of completing the analogy with Tillich's categories concerning art, what of the person who works in a non-religious style with non-religious content? I for my part do not feel that this question needs to be answered, but certainly the "power of being" emerges through the works of such men as well. Perhaps such art is closest to a theology of play, a Dionysian theology.

I believe that while the artist of the grotesque frequently works in a non-religious style, he nonetheless works with religious content. Further, I believe that the eruption of the grotesque in our time is an attack on and a counterbalance to our rationalism and is a renewed call for the recognition of the non-rational as a real and valuable aspect of man and thus, perhaps, of man's experience of God. Perhaps the Stoic was not even half right in locating the link between God and man in reason. Perhaps the grotesque can force us to hear the inaudible word that can speak to us in our vacuum, our time between the times, of new and viable images and symbols which can help to thrust us beyond the bomb and beyond 1984.

It is my hope that the emphases which I have sought to articulate in this work, the combination of ideas and materials which I present, and the sometimes blunt statement of the obvious will stimulate consideration of the limits of reason and the hope beyond these limits.

1

Death Is God

> But what is the philosophy of this generation? Not God
> is dead, that point was passed long ago. Perhaps it should
> be stated that Death is God.   —Saul Bellow, *Herzog*

Without question, one of the most catastrophic evils
visited on modern man was the Nazi death camp. In rig-
idly systematic fashion, in full view of the rest of the
world, with explicit and implicit warnings abounding, in
the midst of peaceful fields and quiet forests, one segment
of humanity reared up veritable factories of destruction
that were to give realization to *Nacht und Nebel,* Night
and Fog, the final solution.

These factories didn't appear instantaneously, fully
developed, from out of nowhere. Alternate solutions
were proposed and discussed and set aside. Bids were let.
Sites were surveyed. There were technical problems to
be solved—Zyklon A, Zyklon B. Slogans were created—
*Reinlichkeit ist Gesundheit; Arbeit macht frei; Jedem
das Seine; Eine Laus dein Tod.*[1] Architects, laboring over

neat drawing boards in tidy rooms, drew up their varied plans—Swiss style, garage style, Japanese style, no style. At the end of their eight hours, the planners went home to their bratwurst and schnapps, and to bouncing their little Heidis and Fritzes on their knees.

The raw material for these factories was gathered from every corner of Europe, even from the shadow of the Vatican. The people, some of whose best friends were Jews—or leftists, or whatever—the people, good Germans, good Czechs, good Frenchmen, turned their heads and convinced themselves that they didn't know what was happening. Against the cries, the rather feeble cries of the victims, those in power here and abroad weighed the options, carefully, like a grocer weighs a hunk of salami or a slab of cheese, and balanced policy decisions against life.

The raw material was loaded into trucks and trains and taken to the factories, where it was subjected to a veritable orgy of careful classification and specialization —the size four female children's shoes here, gold teeth there, brunette hair in this pile, black hair in that, and so on and so on to the tiniest conceivable detail. Then the guards and clerks with a day off would go to the brauhaus for a game of chance and a beery round of "Lilli Marlene." Or maybe they were religious—a good Catholic, a good Lutheran—and might, instead, join their family at the church for a Bach chorale and *corpus meum, sanguis meus*.

For years the processions went into the great belching temples of death at Auschwitz and Dachau and Belsen and Treblinka and Neuengamme and Ravensbruck and Oranienburg in an orgy of worship of the dark god with the empty eyes, great Death himself. The nude votaries were taken to him and offered up, day in, day out.[2]

But 1945 came. The trucks and trains were stopped; the fires went out; the smoke disappeared. Because the processional ended too soon, some staggered away, some of the sacrificial victims, some of the priests. None were guilty, not really—maybe an Ilse Koch here and maybe an Eichmann there. Then, as now, it was soon evident that for society at large it was better not to think of these things; thus Nuremberg became an embarrassment in its own time, not a legend. No one was a Nazi, not really. And no one knew, either here or abroad.

Besides, it is all too difficult to separate out these worshipers of Death from his other devotees in recent times. Four hundred thousand, gathered from all sides, were offered on the fields of Verdun. The rotting flesh in the Nazi factory-temples didn't smell that different from those ex-humans at Verdun or from the roasted, rotting flesh that came out of the nuclear bombing of Nagasaki, or of Hiroshima with its 80,000 offered up in five minutes. Nor, finally, could those dead from the atomic weapons be distinguished from those 130,000 dead in the more "conventional" fire bombing of Dresden—an event we simply chose to leave out of our history books. As Sherman told us, "War is hell"; and as Calley added, "It's no big deal." Or is it perhaps as Bellow said: "Death is God. That is this generation's thought of thoughts"? Death is god, and so it is not strange that presently we name his cultic hardware after the old, gone gods, Atlas and Thor and Nike and Zeus.

Human sacrifice is as much a part of the worship of death today as it ever was in the ancient religions to which we feel so superior. Thus we sacrificed some 50,000 of our own youth to this deity in our recent non-war in Indochina. When that international dispenser of chocolate and chewing gum, the American GI, returned home from his most recent pilgrimage, he told us of the rites in which he had participated.

"I always had this idea of a battalion of little bodies running toward me with rifles and screaming, sneaking around in dark pajamas with daggers. But what you see mainly are civilians, old men, little kids. Once we were on guard at the Dongha Ramp, and for three nights running this little kid, about 3 years old, ran out of his hootch when our truck went by and screamed at us, giving us the finger and saying, 'marines number 10.' It means the worst, the lowest. We decided to rip him off. So the next night we all loaded up with big rocks, I mean like boulders, and when he came out, WHAP, everybody stood up in the truck and threw their rocks and the truck just kept going and I looked back and all I could see was this bloody little hump of flesh, this little bundle of flesh and shorts and blood."

"We were securing artillery out of Route 19 between Pleiku and Ankhe and we were going to test-fire our weapons into the bushes—M-16 rifles and M-60 machine guns. The way we were set up, we were aiming at a village. I knew it, the platoon sergeant knew it and the platoon leader knew it. So I approached them and said, 'You can't fire over there because there's a village there. You're going to hit people.' The sergeant just told me to get away. The lieutenant said, 'So what?' The next day they brought the wounded in. There were 43 at least hurt, I don't know how many killed. I was a medic so I treated the wounded. I called for a helicopter to evacuate them to a hospital and they sent me a truck."

"We got a lot of people killed in Happy Valley, and the first village we hit after that we reconned by fire before we went in. This was Tuyhoa. There were a lot of dead and wounded. The next morning we were camped on a

hill above the village and the villagers were having a
burial ceremony. They hit a guy and people didn't even
look to see if he was dead, they just rolled him over and
put him in the hole with the others and covered him
up." [3]

But the only thing new about the non-war described
in these accounts is that these are not from the transcript
of a war crimes trial but from the mouths of the Winter
Soldiers, those nameless young minions we sent over to
Indochina to be our heroes, returned and refusing to be
heroes, regurgitating, confessing. What they have had to
say has not been too easy to learn about, since the media
has generally seen fit not to give them much coverage;
the original Winter Soldiers Investigations in Detroit
were barely noted. We simply seem unable to register
their agonized confession that, as their spokesman, John
Kerry, said,

> they had personally raped, cut off ears, cut off heads,
> taped wires from portable telephones to human genitals
> and turned up the power, cut off limbs, blown up bodies,
> randomly shot at civilians, razed villages in fashion remi-
> niscent of Genghis Khan, shot cattle and dogs for fun,
> poisoned food stocks and generally ravaged the country-
> side of South Vietnam, in addition to the normal ravage
> of war and the normal and very particular ravaging
> which is done by the applied bombing power of this
> country. . . .
> We fought using weapons against those people which
> I do not believe this country would dream of using were
> we fighting in the European theater [but compare Dres-
> den or Lidice].
> We watched pride allow the most unimportant battles
> be blown up into extravaganzas, because we couldn't lose
> and we couldn't retreat and because it didn't matter how

many American bodies were lost to prove that point, so there were Hamburger Hills and Khe Sans and Hill 18's and Fire Base Sixes, and so many others.

We are here in Washington also to say that the problem of this war is not just a question of war and diplomacy. It is part and parcel of everything that we are trying as human beings to communicate to people in this country—the question of racism, which is rampant in the military, and so many other questions, such as the uses of weapons; the hypocrisy in our taking refuge in the Geneva Conventions and using that as justification for a continuation of this war when we are more guilty than any other body of violations of those Geneva Conventions: in the use of free fire zones, harassment interdiction fire, search and destroy missions, all accepted policy by many units in South Vietnam. . . .

We wish that a merciful God could wipe away our own memories of that service as easily as this Administration has wiped away their memories of us.[4]

Need it be mentioned that their litany went unattended? Our shifts and turns in overt policy in Vietnam scarcely indicate a reaction against the reality of that holocaust. Rather, they illustrate the American desire for a more antiseptic, less intimate means for procuring the same ends we have sought throughout the twenty-five years of our involvement there.

There was no greater possibility that the Winter Soldiers Investigation would remotely realize its aims than that Daniel Ellsberg's action in releasing the Pentagon Papers would achieve the nationwide concern and involvement he hoped for. As Ellsberg has noted, with some alarm, the media did not seek to expose to the public this material and the issues it raises any more than the Government had.

So war is hell. So what else is new? Not much, except

that our litany of death extends, in an increasingly obvious manner, across more and more facets of our lives. Let us use the rubrics of technocracy to support this contention; that is, let us examine numbers and money. In less than a decade, we invested something over one hundred billion dollars in our adventure in Vietnam. At the height of our activities there, this amounted to the following cost schema:

$1,028/second
$61,728/minute
$3,703,704/hour
$88,888,896/day
$622,222,272/week
$2,666,666,880/month
$32,000,000,000/year[5]

Continuing this focus on figures, we note that at this rate at the height of the war the cost per enemy dead (frequently being dead seemed to be the essential criterion in the definition of "enemy") was approximately a quarter of a million dollars each. Continuing the numbers game, we note that we have, over the last several years, invested some thirty billion dollars in missile systems (Hermes, Loki, Thor, Titan, Nike-Ajax, Atlas D, Jupiter, for example) which we have researched, constructed, deployed—and scrapped.

The nature of our priorities falls into stark relief when we consider those needs which were not met during this same period. Housing, health, employment, and educational problems spiraled. A sampling of the oft-recited statistics indicates our failures in the area of welfare:

Of the 7.3 million people on welfare in 1966–1968, 2.1 million were over 65, mostly women (with a median age of 72); 3.5 million were children; 900,000 were mothers

with small children to care for; 700,000 either blind or so
severely handicapped that they couldn't work. There were
only 150,000 males of working age and 100,000 of these
were incapacitated beyond the ability to work or to be
trained.

A person on welfare received an average (it varied by
the state and county) of $1.00 per day for food, an
amount too low for a nutritionally adequate diet. Average benefits for a family of four ranged, state by state,
from a high of $265 a month to a low of $40.

Of the 30 million poor in America in 1969, only one
fourth received welfare funds of any kind.

In the poverty areas of rural America, 70 percent of
the poor families were struggling along on less than
$2,000 a year and one family in every four existed, some-
how, on less than $1,000 a year. One in every 13 houses
in rural America was officially classified as unfit to live in.

The list can, of course, be expanded into other areas.
For example, a comparatively inexpensive $350,000,000
aid to medical education bill was vetoed by the Administration, despite the worsening crisis in our health-care
systems. Repeatedly, bills designed to relieve unemployment have been rejected. The public and the politicians
call for increasingly punitive welfare legislation, based
on a "let them pull themselves up by the bootstraps"
mentality.

Maybe it isn't just war that's hell; maybe peace is hell
also for those on the outside looking in. In America, these
people include such minority groups as Indians and
blacks and Puerto Ricans. Again, theirs is a story that has
been carefully and completely chronicled; it has been
said that as America's crises grow worse, our "reports" on
them (Kerner on "civil disorders," Eisenhower on "violence," etc.) get better. Lower incomes, poorer housing,

poorer and fewer schools, greater unemployment, a higher conviction rate in the courts, a higher casualty rate in Vietnam—these are the bloody facts chronicled in study after study, public and private. Variant understandings of causes and cures seem endless, but the factual aspects of the studies remain monotonously the same.

In addition to and as part of our military ventures, our ordering of natural priorities, and our treatment of minorities, there is our outstanding rape of the physical environment. Again, the reality of our violation of Spaceship Earth is well known, particularly as environmentalism and the ecological issues have passed from the province of a few conservationists and have become a political issue. But it took ten years for us to hear Rachel Carson's *The Silent Spring*; charges that environmentalism is a part of everyman's bogeyman, the Communist Plot, continue and increase particularly during the energy crisis. Also, we still play with hyperbole ("You'd have to eat ten pounds of swordfish every day for seven years and six months before enough mercury would accumulate in your body to give you a good headache") in order to avoid the issues; and, above all, industry and government drag their feet because it has not yet been proved that environmentalism can show a 10 percent profit next year.

The status of people in a culture with the priorities of ours is not difficult to perceive. Man exists to consume—increasingly—in order to sustain increasing production, the vital index in the technological society. Thus that oddball among economists, Thorstein Veblen, noted long ago:

In all the received formulations of economic theory, whether at the hands of the English economists or those of the continent, the human material with which the inquiry is concerned is conceived in hedonistic terms; that is to say, in terms of a passive and substantially inert and immutably given human nature. . . . The hedonistic conception of man is that of a lightning calculator of pleasures and pains, who oscillates like a homogeneous globule of desire of happiness under the impulse of stimuli that shift him about the area, but leave him intact. He has neither antecedent nor consequent. He is an isolated, definitive human datum, in stable equilibrium except for the buffets of the impinging forces that displace him in one direction or another. Self-imposed in elemental space, he spins symmetrically about his own spiritual axis until the parallelogram of forces bears down upon him, whereupon he follows the line of the resultant. When the force of the impact is spent, he comes to rest, a self-contained globule of desire as before. Spiritually, the hedonistic man is not a prime mover. *He is not the seat of a process of living, except in the sense that he is subject to a series of permutations enforced upon him by circumstances external to him and alien to him.*[6]

That is, man is viewed as a thing, mechanistically determined.

What if Western man should, perchance, suffer the transformation from *homo consumens* to a "seat of a process of living"? This must be a horrifying thought for much of American business, but particularly for the advertising industry. A "seat of a process of living" might consider questions such as utility and beauty and nutrition and durability. Planned obsolescence simply would not be bought. Shaker-like simplicity might replace useless chrome and curlicues. Artificial additives that help one to pretend that something tastes good would be dropped. As a by-product of these developments, we might take ecology out of the arena of politics and get serious about our environmental crises.[7] However, it is difficult for us even to envision man today as Veblen's "seat of a process of living."

That man has become a cog in the process of consumption is only part of the picture of the economic aspects of dehumanization in our culture; he is also a cog as a part of the processes of production, particularly via the division of labor. It was Karl Marx, of course, who set forth the classic expression of this hypothesis. Norman Brown notes that for Marx,

> it [the division of labor] is fatal to freedom; it produces the development in a man of one single faculty at the expense of all other faculties, and to subdivide a man's faculties is to kill him; it produces a crippled monstrosity, industrial pathology; intelligence is alienated into the process as a whole while the individual specialist becomes stupid and ignorant. More dispassionately, Durkheim has demonstrated that the division of labor is not a consequence of the individual's search for happiness and does not promote the happiness of the individual; progress, the work of the division of labor, has nothing to do with human happiness.[8]

Thus man, as a cog in the processes of production and consumption, is not considered to be nor is he able to function as a "seat of a process of living." These processes themselves and man within these processes unconsciously, if not consciously, serve not life but the great god, Death.

This godness of Death permeates even our entertainment. For every film such as *A Clockwork Orange* or *Straw Dogs* or *How I Won the War* which grotesques and challenges our orientation toward violence and death, there are ten films such as *The Professionals* and

The Green Berets and *The Dirty Dozen* which feed and succeed on this orientation. Such films are both symptomatic of and contributory to contemporary man's loss of the sense of horror and the concomitant, increasing acceptance of the dominance of death.[9] The euphoria of a death-oriented fatalism spreads.

There should be no need to explain what is meant by the "loss of the sense of horror," for we could have no better illustrations of this phenomenon than those all about us in the United States during the past decade when we became accustomed to our daily after-dinner war on the evening news. Toylike figures from unreal places such as Quang Tri and Kontum twisted and writhed on a twenty-one-inch screen; then, without need for pause or warning, we slid into a Miss America pageant or a toothpaste commercial. One evening we were told to remove small children from the room before we were shown pictures of the trapping of fur-bearing animals in Canada. A week later, *without* warning, we scanned living-color shots of pigs rooting among corpses in a shattered town in Vietnam.

Even when *seemingly* humanitarian motivations do appear activated, they are of dubious success. This is indicated in a general sense by the lack of success of liberal activism over the past decade. A couple of specific examples illustrate and underwrite this fact. *U.S. News & World Report* of November 24, 1969, stated:

> The World Health Organization sent DDT to Borneo to kill mosquitoes. It worked fine. But it didn't kill roaches, which accumulated DDT in their bodies.
>
> Lizards which lived in the thatched huts ate the roaches. The DDT slowed the lizards. Cats then easily caught the lizards. But the cats died. . . .

With the cats gone, rats came, carrying a threat of plague. And with the lizards gone, caterpillars multiplied in the huts, where they fed on the roof thatching. Then the roofs stared caving in.[10]

Similarly, in his 1932 film, *Las Hurdes* (released in English under the title *Land Without Bread*), Luis Buñuel examined the plight of a depressed area in Spain. The peasant people of this area often suffered snakebites, but the bites were not fatal. However, the medicines they used to counteract them were. The people were without cultivable land, so they painstakingly constructed tiny fields. However, the soil would not bear because they had no fertilizers. In the spring, the people were near starvation when the wild cherries began to appear on the trees. The people ate these cherries, but they were still unripe and caused dysentery. Bread was unknown, and although generous teachers sometimes shared theirs with their students, the parents, out of fear and distrust, threw the bread away.

Though most of these illustrations have been drawn from the United States, I hope it is evident that this litany is not a polemic against this country. Rather, most of these illustrations are drawn from our own immediate context because we simply do better what the other peoples, right and left, capitalist and communist, large and small, are seeking to do. However, the arms race, the division of labor, maltreatment of minorities, destruction of the environment, destruction of people, and so on are not the peculiar affliction of the Americans, as some critics would lead us to believe.

George Orwell in his novel *1984* perceptively and prophetically has the whole globe divided up among mega-countries which show no appreciable differences. Each is ruled by the managerial elite which, one suspects, could actually be shifted from one country to another without any considerable disruptions, just as, on a smaller scale, the managerial elite within this country can move about without significant change. Orwell describes his managerial class thus:

> The new aristocracy was made up for the most part of bureaucrats, scientists, technicians, trade-union organizers, publicity experts, sociologists, teachers, journalists, and professional politicians. These people, whose origins lay in the salaried middle class and the upper grades of the working class, had been shaped and brought together by the barren world of monopoly industry and centralized government. As compared with their opposite numbers in past ages, they were less avaricious, less tempted by luxury, hungrier for pure power, and, above all, more conscious of what they were doing and more intent on crushing opposition.[11]

Need one look farther than the Watergate hearings for illustrations?

This managerial elite does not rule; it serves. It serves whatever is the current, accepted ideology of that time and place. But, as is increasingly obvious in the growing sameness that is encircling the globe, this idealism is not an end in itself. It is instead a very flexible rationale bent to the service of systems and machines—that is, the service of the dictates of technology. As will be argued in some detail below, it is rationalism and its offspring, technology, which dominate our time and make dystopia possible, perhaps necessary. And the goal, the telos, of dystopia is death.

What can one conclude but that "Death is God. That is this generation's thought of thoughts."

2

Rationalism, Technique, and Death

Everything that is real, is reasonable.—Hegel

That whore, Reason . . .—Luther

The initial chapter contained an overview of the horrendous, ghastly evidences of the malaise of contemporary culture. This overview is made all the more dreadful by the fact that it is, by now, shopworn and obvious; such descriptions have been offered many times. The still unsettled questions that are the concern of this chapter are: Why this malaise? What has brought us to this state of affairs?

Doomsday books which offer similar descriptions and pose the same questions are among the most common fare for today's reader. They generally follow a pattern something like this: Western civilization, the greatest bash that human history has ever known, is about over. All that's left is the hangover, soon and somber.

These works vary their explanations and emphases as they seek to explain why. The decline of morals, the de-

cline of politics, the decline of education, the inexorable
advance of scientism and technology, the inevitabilities
rooted in man's given biological nature—all these and
more, collectively and individually, are given as cause.[1]

It is significant to note how frequently reason, or the
lack thereof, figures in cause and cure. Volume upon volume has argued around this issue in recent decades.
These works may be divided into two basic groups. For
one group, the roots of our problems rest in the triumph
of unreason; the cure is to be found in some form of reasonable readjustment. For another, smaller group, the
root cause of our problems is reason itself and its triumph
in practical, all-pervasive applications in a technological
society that bends man into the "machineness" of his
tools and systems.[2]

It is with this latter group of works that this study
shares sympathies. Contemporary civilization generally
and Western culture specifically *have* fallen on hard
times, very possibly their last hard times. The plethora of
political solutions—of the right, left, and center—have
not offered any viable hopes. Politics demonstrably does
not lead but follows the hidden presupposition and agen-
das of a culture. Because the basic presuppositions are
shared across ideological and national boundaries, the
variations in political systems have little ultimate significance; Jacques Ellul has made this clear in his work *The
Political Illusion*.

Though there is no basis for optimism, hope is necessary if one is to be human, particularly if one, in any
sense, entertains the possibility of being human in a religious way. Still, hope must not rest in theology and religion as currently practiced, for, as will be indicated in
greater detail below, the vast majority of those who prac-

tice theology and religion in our culture operate within the confines of the same basic presuppositions and structures that have brought us to the current impasse. Bound within these confines, they are unable to break new ground, to offer new and viable solutions.

This study will argue that a primary cause of our malaise is our rationalism, that rationalism whose lineage may be traced from the Platonic myth of the soul with its insistence on the necessary dominance of reason, through the ultimate deification of reason and the emergence of the scientific methodology in the Enlightenment, into the industrialization of the past century and the technological explosion of our own time.

This study will argue that our technological, death-oriented culture has its roots in a rationalism of repression, a repression of the death instinct which then returns to dominate us. Reason seeks to order and structure life in neat, quiet compartments. But life, real life, simply is not neat and orderly. Life is replete with rough edges and fantastic happenings and chances and changes. Since reason cannot accept these challenges to its necessities, reason ultimately opts for death. It is, finally, only that which is dead which is certain to remain quiet and in order. Which reason? What brand of rationalism?—it makes no difference. Always they all must end in death. "Death is God. That is this generation's thought of thoughts."

On Reason and Rationalism

As we move into consideration of these arguments, a clarification of terms is necessary. First, an abstract definition of terms is offered, but as the chapter proceeds the terms will, we hope, take on flesh and blood through illustrations and examples.

Throughout, reference has been made to reason and rationalism. By rationalism is meant that position which holds that the essence of man and the key to all meaningful understanding of man and his place in the cosmos is reason. By reason is meant not simply man's capacity for thought nor his ability to carry on cognitive activity. Rather, "to reason" as the term is used here is to submit truth and reality before the bar of the abstract principles of non-contradiction (it is not possible for something to be and not be at the same time) and necessity (what is, is necessarily). Rationalism is that mode of being which elevates reason thus armed to the position of dominance in the affairs of men and gods.

Truth comes to be that which "fits" logically and neatly within those "essential" structures imposed on being by our determination to abstract and generalize from the first principles of non-contradiction and necessity. But, committed to these principles, we become blind to the reality that we have no Archimedean point from which we can determine just what the essential structures are. Nor, without resort to physical or psychological violence, have we been able to gain a consensus concerning just what is logical and neat.

Thus the story of Western man has been the story of his hidden presuppositions, often rooted in the subconscious and held wholistically rather than rationally, controlling his use of his soldiers, non-contradiction and necessity. And the basic presupposition, denied, fumigated, glossed over and camouflaged though it may be, is the desire to control, to run life and guarantee it on one's own terms. Via reason man would be as God, knowing good and evil, and enforcing his knowledge on others.

The ancient and time-honored principle of non-contradiction insists that if one proposition is true, its opposite is surely false. If something is black, it cannot be white; if there is a mountain, there must be a valley. The principle in itself in the abstract looks innocent enough, but it presupposes the Archimedean point from which one may determine the universals. Neglected is the reality that men at their wisest and most selfless may disagree concerning what, precisely, is contradictory. Since the principle itself is flawed, the capacity for disaster is obvious; since the principle is generally hidden and unexamined, the capacity for disaster is magnified. Our history tells the story.

Typically, if this principle is questioned or if different understandings of the "essentials" emerge, violence and/or unreason ensues. Thus the gentle slave-philosopher Epictetus threatened to cut off the nose of his master, who would not accept the principle of non-contradiction. Epictetus argued that the very basis of the ability to distinguish between noses and whiskers was lost to the man who would not accept this principle. Leibnitz, the equally brilliant seventeenth-century philosopher, resorted to the *argumentum ad hominem*, the nasty personal remark, against Descartes when Descartes suggested that there perhaps could be mountains without valleys— even though he couldn't perceive just how. For the rationalist, the principle of non-contradiction is not to be questioned because, if it is, *everything* is open to question. *Man's control of certainty is lost.*

The principle of necessity insists that if the weight of logic requires that such and such a proposition is factually correct, it is also necessary. All reasonable men will agree. The matter of goodness or badness does not enter. Thus the principle of necessity would free reason and truth from both the confines of ethics and the messiness of human suffering.

Thus Aristotle insisted that "necessity does not allow itself to be persuaded." On the whole, it would be better to execute a mad dog than Socrates, but if the necessities of impersonal facts insisted, then Socrates must drink the hemlock.

> Corrupters of the youth of Athens must be executed.
> Socrates is a corrupter of the youth of Athens.
> Therefore, Socrates must be executed.

One could wish otherwise, but, alas, necessity does not allow itself to be persuaded—even though necessity will allow one to avoid the issue concerning what it means to corrupt Athens' youth.

Non ridere, non lugere, neque detesteri, sed intelligere, said Spinoza. "Don't laugh, don't weep, don't hate; just understand." In present society this admonition emerges in the constant call for objectivity which has become a well-nigh universal banner wherever problems or thoughts are to be examined or decisions are to be made. Again, it is assumed that man can and must be dominated by reason; again, it is assumed that man, via reason, does have access to an Archimedean point. Thus Joffre during his time of command in World War I could insist that he not be subjected to the sight of battlefront casualties because they might cloud his objectivity so that he would not make the right and reasonable decision—like the decision to hold the Verdun salient at all costs. Thus also a Nazi officer at Treblinka could condemn the commandant of the camp for unobjective, emotional enjoyment of the slaughter of the inmates which resulted in inefficiency; only the objective and reasonable man could determine how to kill the most people quickest. It is the same brand of "rational objectivity" which permeates the managerial councils of business and education and government throughout the Muzak society.

Nor has religion, for all its talk of concepts such as faith and revelation, escaped from the dominance of rationalism. Thus, for example, Aquinas could state: "Only that is *excluded from the divine omnipotence* which contradicts the reason or essence of being, that is, that something at the same time be and not be; and something . . . not have been that has been." [3] Similarly, the First Vatican Council decreed: "Even if faith be above reason, there still can never be any real disagreement between faith and reason, since the same God who reveals mysteries and infuses faith has endowed the human soul with the light of reason. God, however, cannot negate himself, nor can truth ever contradict truth."

Obviously, deism was a form of religion that openly embraced the principles of rationalism. However, while this has not been so readily recognized, orthodox Christianity and its reactionary element, fundamentalism, and most of the more liberal attempts for relevance which are lumped together under the label of neo-orthodoxy also function within the confines of rationalism. They are alike in their quest for the god that can be pointed out as the right god, the reasonable god, the god that all reasonable men will accept.

As Anders Nygren has pointed out, orthodox Christianity rests on a rationalistic understanding of such key concepts as "gospel" and "revelation" and "faith." Nygren says:

For instance, the word "gospel" has been interpreted as if
it meant only a doctrine or the proclamation of timeless
religious truths. "The righteousness of God" is presented
as a static attribute in the divine nature. "Revelation" is
thought of as the theoretical communication of formerly
hidden knowledge. And by "faith" is meant the affirmation and acceptance of this doctrine, of such universally
valid religious ideas.[4]

Thus today also, for example, the hyper-orthodox theologian Francis A. Schaeffer, in his *Escape from Reason,*
condemns all challenges to the efficacy of reason and em-
phasizes that "man's aspiration for the validity of reason
is well founded. If a certain thing is true, i.e., according
to rational criteria its opposite is not true." [5] Like Aristotle, Schaeffer sees all things, all beings, even God himself, capitulating to the necessary truths of reason and its
first principles.

For the rationalist, theological or otherwise, reason says
all. The answer to the old conundrum is indelibly clear:
God, the God who is understood to have created and
bound himself to the principles of reason, *cannot* make a
stone so big that he can't lift it. But as Kierkegaard has
pointed out: "The god understood is no god. The god
that can be pointed out is an idol, and the religiosity that
makes an outward show is an imperfect form of religiosity. And talk of this god is only so much twaddle."

From the time of Plato and Aristotle on through the
present, rationalism has dominated our understanding of
man and gods and the cosmos. From the Enlightenment
onward, this rationalistic approach to reality has emerged
victorious in both the secular and the religious sphere.
Via its stepchild, the scientific methodology, it has given
birth to the managerial technocracy we have today.

But rationalism is a disastrous mode of being because its first principles of non-contradiction and necessity and its supposition of an Archimedean point are more than inadequate; they are dangerous and deadly. To function out of these rationalistic perceptions means that either one must close one's eyes to major portions of reality or else, more typically, one must bend time and effort to making reality behave in accord with the abstract model one has fashioned via these perceptions.

Rationalism is a negative mode of being because it involves a drastically one-sided view of man. Man is not simply reason, a kind of brain on legs; rather, man is a complex of reasons and will and emotion, of the conscious and the subconscious, of ego and id. When reason is made the charioteer instead of simply a partner in juxtaposition with the other factors in the total complex that constitutes man, we are in as dangerous a position as when we approach an iceberg assuming that what is visible is all we have to reckon with.

Reason is a *part* of man; this aspect of man must be heard, given its due.[6] While there are inherent dangers in treating the rational consciousness as a differentiated psychic function, as was first done by Plato, this may at times in the life of the individual or the history of the race be beneficial. But to conceive of truth as the domain of the purely rational is to move from respect for the rational to capitulation to it; this is rationalism.

As reason must be given its due, so also are science, its methodology, and its "knowledge" to be appreciated. In fact, their penultimate value and their practical significance for everyday life should be obvious. However, rationalism has fostered in the popular imagination in our culture a pervasive absolutizing of scientific knowledge and methodology, in spite of the fact that scientific achievement has frequently brought mixed blessing.

Further, the underlying presuppositions behind scientific achievement are not infrequently arbitrarily chosen and changeable, not proven by experience or by inviolable absolutes, as the man in the street often assumes. A simple and effective illustration of the fact that the scientist chooses among possible sets of presuppositions that are themselves without factual, empirical certitude is offered in the case of Einstein's theory of relativity. On the basis of the principles of simplicity and economy, Einstein *chose* to use the geometry of Georg Reimann rather than that of Euclid or Lobachevski or anyone else. However, simplicity and economy are theoretical principles, not facts of experience.[7]

That the four-dimensional universe does not come to us as an established absolute of observation and experience does not, of course, invalidate it. However, an illustration such as this should help to remind us that rationalistic "truths" in actuality are selected by reason, often on the basis of unexamined presuppositions, from among other options. These "truths" are not foreordained, eternally fixed absolutes. This is not news to the scientist, of course; Heisenberg's study of indeterminacy, for example, has done more than contemporary religion to remind us of the limits of science.

But such truths as "Necessity does not allow itself to be persuaded" may be opposed not only on the grounds of their dubious roots in observation and experience. More significantly, they must be opposed on the grounds that they bend, fold, mutilate people; in Shestov's words, they are "soulless and indifferent." It is such soulless indifference that allowed the very correct choice of Zyklon

B over Zyklon A without asking *why* Zyklon anyway—
or final solutions or *Lebensraum* or anything of the kind.
It is the same soulless indifference which allows the logic
of paying millions to some people in this country for not
growing food while permitting other people in this same
country to die of starvation and malnutrition. A thousand more examples of the consequences of rationalism
and its soulless indifference are ready at hand.

As Shestov wrote, "Reason, by its very nature, hates life
more than anything in the world, feeling it instinctively
to be its irreconcilable enemy." [8] Yet, according to the
Enlightenment and the current rationalistic technocracy
which is its offspring, it is the "truths" of reason which
are to make us noble and free.

Technique

Our culture in general has not only blindly accepted
rationalism but has also placed the highest value on technology as reason's finest gift to mankind and our key hope
for a better future. It is commonly assumed that reason
has given us technology and that technology affords man
the tools for building a better world. The basic decisions
and directions of our culture clearly indicate that the
overwhelming majority of people, including particularly
the "leaders" of our managerial society, have no serious,
penetrating reservations about technology.

Though with little lasting effect, there have been several searching critiques of technology during the past
decades. These diverse works include studies such as Gie-
dion's *Mechanization Takes Command* and Mumford's
*Technics and Human Development: The Myth of the
Machine,* films such as Chaplin's *Modern Times* and

Antonioni's *Red Desert,* and novels such as Capek's *R.U.R.* and Orwell's *1984.* However, the most thorough and absolute condemnation of technology is Jacques Ellul's *The Technological Society* which traces the very roots of our malaise into technology and technique.

Ellul's analysis is exhaustive and his annihilation of the cheap hope that is typically vested in technology is devastating; his work must be given much more careful consideration than it has received thus far. At this point in our study an examination of his critique of our culture can help us perceive more fully the exact nature of our crisis with its unholy alliance between reason and death.

A very brief summary of the highlights of Ellul's understanding of our technological society follows. According to Ellul, contemporary culture is encased within the artificial, non-traditional, non-historical environment of technique. Technique is defined as *"the totality of methods rationally arrived at and having absolute efficiency in every field of human activity."* [9] It is to be stressed that, in Ellul's thought, technique is not simply equated with technology nor with machines; these are seen as driven by technique but not as synonomous with it.

For Ellul, the relationship between technique and society has a radically different character in the post-Enlightenment era. Prior to this time, some human choice was allowed in the technical processes, technique varied between different areas, and the understanding of human progress was not bound to technical progress; that is, technique existed, but within boundaries. Since that time, however, technique has advanced in such fashion that none of these limits any longer are viable. Instead, technique has encompassed all aspects of life; it forms our primary environment. In our technological society, the means have become the ends, and the qualitative orientation of primitive technology has been superseded by the quantitative orientation of modern technique.

The two primary characteristics of modern technique, according to Ellul's analysis, are its rationality and its artificiality. Rationality dominates; out of it issue the mechanics that thwart the spontaneous and the individualistic. Administration with its techniques is the acme of this rationality; its goal is the endless classification and "pigeonholing" which becomes an end in itself. Artificiality is contrasted with naturalness. The natural *is* spontaneous and individualistic; since technique cannot abide this, it replaces naturalness with artificiality. The artificial imposition of technique spirals with a resulting irreversible progression away from nature. The goal of the technological society is to adjust people to this artificiality.

Ellul also describes several secondary characteristics of modern technique. One of these is the automatism of its processes; human choice is removed. Man can only "decide in favor of the technique that gives the maximum efficiency." [10] If something can be done, it must be done; if something is made, it must be used. Another secondary characteristic is the self-augmentation of technique without any significant interruption by the human factor. Technique necessitates technique which feeds on technique. Third, technique is monistic; it is everywhere the same. There is no such thing as good or bad technique; technique does not allow moral judgments. "In a sound evaluation of the problem, it ought to be said: on the one side, technique; on the other side, abuse of it. There are different techniques which correspond to different neces-

sities. But all techniques are inseparably united. . . .
Not even a moral conversion of technicians would make
a difference. At best, they would cease to be good technicians." [11] A fourth important secondary characteristic of
modern technique is universalism; there is an inherent
drive in technique to subsume *all* under its principles.

The god of technique is efficiency; it is the "necessary
truth" which dominates technique, the environment of
modern life. To efficiency, man has sold his soul. Efficiency is not to be questioned, but to be served, totally,
always.

According to Ellul, hope for improvement via political
processes is illusory in our technological society. Old nations as well as new, communism as well as capitalism,
democracies as well as dictatorships are all subsumed
under technique with its drive for efficiency. Not only
has this happened in the political arena, nationally and
internationally, but also all facets of life have been politicized; all tensions are politicized. Thus this dominance
of technique has spread like a cancer over these forces
which might commonly be thought to be the means for
restructuring our society. This, coupled with the universal state control of the media, renders political revolution an impossibility.

But the loss of "humanness" before the onrush of technique and the totalitarian state which embodies it will
in the end be painless.

> The edifice of the technical society will be completed. It
> will not be a universal concentration camp, for it will be
> guilty of no atrocity. It will not seem insane, for every-
> thing will be ordered, and the stains of human passion
> will be lost amid the chromium gleam. We shall have
> nothing more to lose, and nothing to win. Our deepest

instincts and our most secret passions will be analyzed, published, and exploited. We shall be rewarded with everything our hearts ever desired. And the supreme luxury of the society of technical necessity will be to grant the bonus of useless revolt with an acquiescent smile.[12]

In the face of this deeply disturbing view of our present and future, Ellul offers only an either-or. One can either capitulate to the totalitarianism of technique (to oppose this via political struggle is illusory) or seek "the emergence of social, political, intellectual or artistic bodies, associations, interest groups or economic or Christian groups totally independent of the state, yet capable of opposing it, able to reject its pressures as well as its controls, and even its gifts." [13] The one hope on this side of an apocalyptic eschatology is life independent of the state and independent of technique.

The evidence that Ellul amasses is formidable and his analysis is frighteningly thorough and consistent. It is much easier to try to tag him with a label—"new Manichean," or simply "pessimist"—than it is to refute him. The warnings he gives us are critically important and frequently beyond argument.

Still, however much one must agree with Ellul's observations, particularly concerning the dominance of technique and the illusion of politics, there is room for questions and modifications, and these may help clarify both our problems and our possibilities.

First, are there really essential differences between ancient technique and modern technique? Ellul's discussion of the rationality of modern technique which issues in an administration with its registration and pigeonholing of people reminds one of a most ancient series of objections to administrations; that is, the objections which

Samuel raises in I Samuel, ch. 8, against the establishment of a monarchy in Israel. Or one can think back to
the purposes and uses of the Roman census. Further, as
Vahanian says in an article that is most appreciative of
Ellul, Ellul seems to be in danger of a kind of abstract
separation of Christ the Lord from Christ the Savior. The
follower of Christ the Lord might be able to take a spectator view of the world's fallenness. However, the individual who would live out his entanglement with the
Christ who is also Savior of this chaotic world can scarcely
avoid descending from the spectator role into the messy
arena of life.

> Descending into the arena may involve the difficult busi-
> ness of political choice in spite of the severe limits on
> hope of significant change, even in spite of hopelessness
> in this action. The purpose of such action finally may not
> be hope of change but nothing more nor less than affir-
> mation of humanness.[14]

Also, isn't technique capable of good and bad uses? For
example, there are not simply police techniques that are
everywhere applied the same; it would seem experiential
that there are police who use their techniques to good
ends and those who use them to bad ends. The charge of
monism of technique seems somewhat escapist, even if
one grants the current dominant ruthlessness in the use
of technique. Technique in our culture *is* swallowed up
in service of war, not peace; ultimately it is in the service
of death, not life. But it is critically important that we
push on to ask for the ultimate roots of this universally
destructive *application* of technique. Ellul himself seems
to do this when he states in his more theologically oriented analysis of our crisis, *The Presence of the Kingdom*:

> The will of the world is always a will to death, a will to suicide. We must not accept this suicide, and we must so act that it cannot take place. So we must know what is the actual form of the world's will to suicide in order that we may oppose it, in order that we may know how, and in what direction, we ought to direct our efforts.[15]

What must be stressed, as Ellul does here, is that the ultimate question is not that concerning the *form* of the world's will to suicide but rather the question after the *roots* of that will, a will that has existed throughout human history but has only recently bent the tool of technique to itself. As Ellul himself notes, technique in ancient times was qualitatively oriented, and was not "demonic."

Finally, must one accept Ellul's key argument concerning the dominance of efficiency, equally, in all social applications of technique? There is considerable evidence that in the final analysis efficiency does not dominate our technological society. Christopher Lasch, for example, points out that neither the airplane nor the automobile is the most efficient means available to us. Lasch states:

> Even from a purely technical point of view, it would make more sense to restore an efficient system of rail transport than to continue to build airports and highways that will be obsolete by the time they are completed. (It is precisely this anticipated obsolescence, however, that makes them attractive.) [16]

However, it is not the air industry, propped up by the military market, which precludes development of a more efficient transportation system; it is the automobile industry. The energy crisis underlines this reality. Lasch notes that the state, both in America and in Western Europe, has chosen to subsidize the automotive interests at the expense of other forms of transportation.[17] This is done in spite of the fact that more efficient transportation systems are available and in spite of the negative effect of the automobile on the environment. The abstract concept of efficiency does not explain such actions.

Further, air warfare is generally vastly inefficient; this is pointed out even by a CIA report included in the Pentagon Papers. Chemical-biological warfare, a technique developed but seldom used, would be much more efficient. Lasch suggests that air warfare as we have practiced it in Vietnam

> is not necessarily the most efficient method of mass destruction, but it is the most *expensive* method of mass destruction. That is its great advantage from the point of view of advanced capitalist society—a society, that is, which thrives on the production of unnecessary commodities. War, obviously, is the purest form of waste and aerial warfare is the most wasteful method of war.[18]

While there is much of critical value in Ellul's analysis, he underemphasizes the responsibility of the individual before technique, overemphasizes the differences between past and present uses of technique, and he does not adequately account for the tremendous inefficiency of our technological society. The inadequacies of his analysis stem from his failure to pursue and emphasize the origins of the misapplication of technique. These origins are in rationalism, as defined and discussed above. Technique as practiced in our culture is nothing more than the handmaiden, the tool, of rationalism. In technique as established in the post-Enlightenment period, rationalism has the tool whereby, at last, its dominance might be established unchallenged.

The causes and the possible cure of our malaise are grasped only as we focus on this monism and universalism of rationalism *and then pursue its ultimate psychological and theological roots*. In the passage above from *The Presence of the Kingdom*, Ellul himself indicates these roots when he says: "The will of the world is always a will to death, a will to suicide." Rationalism, with its powerful tool, technique, roots ultimately in "the will to death."

Death

As a radical social critic, Freud (whom theologians have been too quick either to condemn or to baptize) pursued the question concerning what it was, what forces at the border of the biological and the "spiritual," which propelled our culture on what he perceived to be a downward spiral.[19] Both in the method and the nature of his quest Freud sought to move beyond the traditional subject-object dualism and in so doing moved into his attempts to understand the dualism of instincts within the subject. As is well known, in the evolution of his thought Freud moved from the antithesis of sex (eros) and self-preservation (ego instinct, hunger) to the antithesis of sex and aggression or love and hate, to his final position, the dualism of the life instinct and the death instinct. Sex versus self-preservation, sex versus aggression, life versus death—it is the final antithesis which was the conclusion of Freud's quest, and the basis of the pessimism which marked his final years.

As we concern ourselves with this reality of the dominance of death and the question of the possibility of breaking this dominance, we would do well to consider the insights that are offered by Freud and those who have built on his understandings of this central dualism. Freud's hypothesis of a life instinct and a death instinct as universal aspects of living creatures can be a helpful conceptual tool in explaining and treating psychopathological cases. Also, if one extends these instincts to a corporate level, it is possible that one may be afforded insights into the destructive tendencies of our culture.

By a life instinct is meant the inherent tendency of that which lives to maintain and continue its life at all costs. Each of us can think of many illustrations of the powerful wish of that which lives to continue to do so.

However, we tend to find the hypothesis of a death instinct much more objectionable. Our immediate response is to deny this as implausible, contrary to reason and experience, except in the rather rare case of the suicide. Freud, nevertheless, argued that the death instinct is as real as the life instinct and is just as much a part of the fundamental instinctual apparatus of each person.

Pressing man's history back toward the womb and pressing his theory of instincts to its basics, Freud was able to explain and treat the realities of repression and self-destruction on the basis of this fundamental dualism. Man has not only an instinct to experience the adventures of life but also an instinct for release from the ceaseless pummeling that such adventures cause him. At the borders of the biological and the spiritual in his makeup, man is in quest not only of life but also of escape from it. He seeks a return to the quiet of the womb; lacking this possibility, he seeks the quiet of death. For Freud, these instincts are innate; they are fundamental.

Via the positing of a death instinct, one can readily explain self-destructive tendencies such as masochism; perhaps one may even posit a corporate analogy. But what of such phenomena as sadism, or, on a corporate level, death camps and wars? Such phenomena are an extroversion of the death wish. The desire to die is transformed into the desire to kill. This provides a release from the self-destructive tendencies, a mode of balance for the life instinct. This dualism of instincts is fundamental to Freud's understanding of "the demands made upon the mind in consequence of its connection with the body." Repression is the force of the death instinct over the life instinct.[20]

According to Freud, the dominance of death and the will to suicide portrayed in the initial chapter roots deep within, in these instincts, in the dualism of life *against* death wherein death increasingly gains the upper hand. Both in terms of its inevitability and its power, it is the stronger. These are the roots of the pessimism of Freud's later years in which he seems to have radically questioned the possibility of mental health.

It is not, as Ellul suggests, efficiency which is god in our rationalistic, technological society, but death. "Death is God. That is this generation's thought of thoughts." However, this is not a novelty of the modern world; rather, it is simply that, given the tools we possess today, the ability of other thoughts to compete is decimated. The corporate will to death, the will to suicide, is finally capable of realization on a corporate scale. The sole meaningful question for us today is this: Can this dominance of death, this will to suicide, be broken?

Psychoanalysts after Freud generally have not maintained the rigors of his vision but have moved toward the instinctual monism of Jung or, more frequently, have acquiesced to returning the "maladjusted" to the death-dominated culture from which they have withdrawn.

Freud, the radical social critic, has been mutilated into an apostle of adjustment.

This transformation, like the rationalisms of the theologians and like the illusory practice of politics, does little to refute the reality of Freud's ultimate and simple antithesis. As Norman Brown notes, both the logic and the empirical data are formidable. In Chapter 1, I reviewed evidence of this dominance of death in our time. At this point, I would like to push this evidence farther, relating the instinctual clash to the directions of our culture and to the dominance of rationalism, *a rationalism of repression*.

There is much in our culture which becomes intelligible on the basis of the Freudian instinctual antithesis of life and death. On this basis, the Nazi social repression that peaked in their effort against the Jews and issued in the death camps "makes sense." If the ultimate Nazi goal was victory, the repression that led to the mass exodus of intellectuals such as Albert Einstein, Walter Gropius, Paul Tillich, Hans Morgenthau, Thomas Mann, Otto Klemperer, Bertolt Brecht, George Grosz, Hannah Arendt, Bruno Walter, Erich Fromm, Arnold Schoenberg, and many others is obviously counterproductive. Victory would require the use of these people; they could be disposed of later. Likewise, the effort, the money, the cost in every sphere, which went into *Nacht und Nebel*, Night and Fog, the Nazis' "final solution," was counterproductive if the quest was for victory. It was counterproductive not because it roused ire against Germany (*which it did not do*), but because men, machines, and goods that could have been put into the war instead went into the obscene extermination of critically vital resources, minds and muscles.[21] Nazi Germany was not so much a victim of conquest or of blunders, but of suicide. The will of the world and the reasoning of the world is a will to death, a reasoning to death, to suicide.

Thus also the priorities evidenced in the United States over the past few years are suicidal—100 billion dollars plus for a lost war, but a veto for an inexpensive aid to medical education bill; 30 billion dollars for scrapped missile systems, but no school lunches in the Mississippi delta; a loan of a quarter of a billion dollars to Lockheed, but a pervasive acceptance of the punitive Reagan welfare proposals; six billion dollars for ABM, but a token to environmental concerns; and so on and on and on. So also education on the primary, secondary, and higher levels, instead of attaining wisdom and creativity and health—or even the adjustment it seeks—issues in the most obvious incoherencies and in chaos. Similarly our penal system, at considerable expense, produces 70 to 80 percent recidivism because we focus on punishment as an end in itself, a kind of corporate sadism, even though effective rehabilitative procedures and possibilities exist. All of this is so senseless—unless the guiding sense is death.

One can move from such specific examples into a more theoretical consideration of our culture and examine the nature of society and religion, the Protestant ethic, the money complex, and purposiveness in general and find staggering support for the same conclusion. Such an analysis is Norman Brown's *Life Against Death,* a thorough and carefully documented study of our culture; these pages are obviously indebted to his brilliant work. Brown states:

> Repression generates the instinctual compulsion to change the internal nature of man and the external world in

which he lives, thus giving man a history and subordinating the life of the individual to the historical quest of the species. . . . Men huddle into hordes as a substitute for parents, to save themselves from independence, from "being left alone in the dark." Society was not constructed, as Aristotle says, for the sake of life and more life, but from defect, from death and the flight from death, from fear of separation and fear of individuality.[22]

One is reminded of Dostoevsky's "The Legend of the Grand Inquisitor" with its insight that man is ever in flight from freedom and responsibility for himself in his quest for answers, any answers, secured outside the self.

Institutional religion—about the only brand available to the man in the street—is the sanctification of that flight, that quest. Further, religion as practiced in the prevailing orthodoxies with their *ordo salutis*, their steps of salvation, and their easy, domesticated god, concludes that flight in a cheap and airy immortality. There is no more Yahweh who will be what he will be, who *kills* as well as *makes alive;* rather, the god of orthodoxy and its kin, fundamentalism and much of neo-orthodoxy and the theology of hope, is the simplistic guarantor of a life which is non-life—thus the twaddle of so much God-talk.[23]

The origin, nature, and direction of the money complex also supports Freud's contention and illustrates our plight. Drawing on Marx, Veblen, Durkheim, Herskovits, Schumpeter, and others, Brown persuasively sketches out the anality of the money complex and its roots in the death instinct. Economic activity in general and especially the economic organization of capitalism are cultural substitutes for lost infantile pleasures, Brown argues, and shows with devastating clarity the instinctual psychological roots of such activity. Building on these thinkers, Brown traces the roots of the alienated consciousness into the compulsion to work. The compulsion to work is entangled with and generates the loss of the consciousness of the self as a locus of worth. Instead, worth is located in things or in money as an abstract representative of things; the more one has of things and money, the more his supposed worth. An abstraction, economic man, replaces the concrete human being, and this abstraction dehumanizes human nature. Brown writes:

> In this dehumanized human nature man loses contact with his own body, more specifically with his senses, with sensuality and with the pleasure-principle. And this dehumanized human nature produces an inhuman consciousness, whose only currency is abstractions divorced from real life—the industrious, coolly rational, economic, prosaic mind. Capitalism has made us so stupid and one-sided that objects exist for us only if we can possess them or if they have utility.[24]

Unlike Hegel, Marx, Nietzsche, Freud, and so many others, Brown argues that the villain in the human malaise is not an external force such as the "Primal Father" or the bourgeoisie. It is not an external force which can or should constrain man under its domination. Thus a revolution of whatever sort cannot be effective. It will not suffice to "expropriate the expropriators," says Brown, for "the slave is in love with his own chains." Brown is right; this is the ultimate crossroads not only in social theory but also in the concrete, mundane affairs of men and nations.

From within, man is compelled to work superfluously. *He has rejected* the ability to distinguish what he needs from the superfluous. His basic necessity is food, but under the guise of cloudy assertions about economic necessity, within the money complex he comes to attribute to that which is not food and is not necessary the worth of food; in the Freudian formula, "excrement becomes aliment." [25]

Via Brown's analysis, our society's amazing inefficiency and waste (which Ellul's focus on technique and efficiency neglects and which Marx attributes to capitalism) becomes intelligible. Waste is part of the game in our death-oriented culture; thus how fitting the use of "waste" for "kill" in the jargon of the Vietnam war.

In an effort to regain the possibility of meaningful talk of "salvation," Brown makes a subtle shift from the Freudian ontology of instinctual dualism to what he calls instinctual dialectics.[26] Freud's instinctual dualism (life against death) accounts for the continuity between man and the animals and thus, though metaphysical, roots the understanding of man squarely in biological principles. However, this Freudian dualism does not leave room for a discontinuity between man and animals, understands the instinctual conflict as a "necessary truth" (really a biological necessity) rather than a human aberration, and can end only in a consistent and thoroughgoing pessimism.

Arguing particularly from a pre-ambivalent instinctual stage in infancy, Brown maintains that instinctual ambivalence is a human prerogative. This polarity of the life-death instincts exists also in animals, but not in ambivalence. The basis of human neurosis, cultural and individual, is the development of conflict in the polarities. "Man is the animal which has separated into conflicting opposites the biological unity of life and death, and has then subjected the conflicting opposites to repression." [27]

It is not death but the repression of death, the impossible flight from death, which is the ultimate origin of our cultural malaise. Death itself is the foundation of individuality: "[Even] at the simplest organic level, any particular plant or animal has its own uniqueness and individuality because it lives its own life and no other—that is to say, because it dies." [28] However, man represses death and loses his individuality in a social history that is essentially sick.

Again, it is not reason per se which is "bad," but it is reason in the service of repression (or "quantifying rationality," to use Brown's term) which circles out in flight from death and back in obeisance to it. That is, the use of reason to foster the post-infantile ambivalence or conflict of the fundamental polarity of instincts which *need not* be locked in their combat results in the dominance of death. Rationalism is reason in the bondage of death. As the most malleable of the materials caught up in this unnecessary combat, reason becomes the key link in the union of the slave with his chains. The impossible flight from death dictates that use of reason which is the rationalism we have examined previously.

> The flight is impossible, for the incapacity to accept death activates a regressive death wish; it also contaminates Eros and burdens the projects of infantile narcissism with the flight from death. As a result of instinctual ambivalence, the history of childhood is the history of an organism caught in an ever widening sequence of dualisms which it vainly seeks to overcome, till in the end, after a final climactic struggle, it acknowledges defeat and acquiesces in its own permanent impairment. In this sequence of dualisms we can trace the steps by which the

death instinct is transformed into a principle of active
negativity.[29]

The life instinct itself is overshadowed and ultimately
defeated not by death but by man's impossible efforts to
repress the death instinct. Reason in the service of repression kills and/or commits suicide; given the technological
capacities and the dominance of technique in our era,
the difference becomes academic.

It is not fortuitous that the ancient Yahwist who
penned the second and third chapters of Genesis contrasted the tree of knowledge and the tree of life: "Original sin [is] the knowledge that what is is necessarily." [30]
The telos of such knowledge is death. "Its narrowness, its
lack of imagination, its preoccupation with 'objectivity'
and its wish to extrude from thought all human emotion, its conviction that there is nothing in the world that
is essentially and forever mysterious and rationally in-
explicable, its refusal to even entertain the possibility of
a universe in which the rules of tradition (such as principles of non-contradiction and identity) do not hold
sway—all this condemns it to sterility." [31]

"And you will be as gods, knowing good and evil."
Sterile systems of knowledge of good and evil, powerless
in the face of death, perversely twisted into the service
of death—these are the highest accomplishments of our
rationalism. Let us not return to the reconsideration of
her lesser achievements. In the kingdoms of the knowledge of good and evil, death is god, and technology is reason's ministrant ensuring death's worship.

3

Beyond Rationalism

The question is, Can theology contribute to the quest to move beyond this rationalism which is a subtle worship of death? Though the vast majority of theologizing, theoretical and practical, in study and in congregation, is done in the rationalistic mode, in our traditions, from the earliest times through to the present, there is a powerful and fascinating continuum of men who would indeed call us beyond reason. Let us consider this continuum and the direction it offers to our own troubled times.

Non-Rationalistic Theology

In Genesis 32:22–32 there is that curious story of Jacob at the Jabbok with the account of his wrestling match with the deity. Out of this struggle, Jacob receives a new name: "Your name shall no more be called Jacob, but Israel, for you have striven with God." This change in name is, of course, of the utmost significance, because for the ancient Hebrews a name was not a label picked at random, but rather a summarization of what one was all about; thus, for example, "Elijah," meaning "Yahweh is my God." In Genesis, ch. 32, Jacob becomes Israel; a new identity is established. Then, at the end of the dialogue in this passage, Israel asks the deity, "What is your name?" The deity's response, even more clearly than the struggle preceding, marks out the distinction between God and man with that abrupt concluding question: "Why do you ask?" Even the possibility of the rationalistic twaddle that Kierkegaard speaks of is closed off here; the naming of the deity is not given to man. God is not known via propositional statements and reasons; rather, God is known only in events—often strange and violent events at that.

In the story of Moses and the burning bush in Exodus, ch. 3, a name is given, but it is a name so totally different from "Unmoved Mover" or the catechetical description of the Omniscient, Omnipotent, Omnipresent Etcetera.[1] The name is Yahweh, a form of the Hebrew "to be" verb which may be translated as a present ("I am who I am"), a future ("I will be what I will be"), or a causative ("I am the one who causes what happens to come to pass"). It is obvious that none of these translations would allow man to pocket God within his reason, for this God is met and known only in events.

Further, he is the God who can turn up even in those events man considers most unlikely. Thus the prophet cries out in astonishment, "Who has believed our report?" (Isa. 53:1) as he marvels at his inconceivable insight that this God is met not in power, as man would consider reasonable, but in weakness, in suffering. This is totally unreasonable.

It is the same God who rules in the kingdom that Jesus thrusts before men: "The kingdom of God is not coming with signs to be observed; nor will they say, 'Lo, here it is!' or 'There!' for behold, the kingdom of God is in the midst of you" (Luke 17:20–21). The God who rules via the march of armies makes sense as men count history; for those who have given up on sense in history, the God of the apocalypse will appear and vindicate the reasonableness of their beliefs and actions. But for Jesus, he is met in none of these places or ways. He is instead, unreasonably, among us here, in the messiness of now.

Paul also knows little of the God of reason: "For it is written, I will destroy the wisdom of the wise, and will bring to nothing the understanding of the prudent. . . . For the Jews require a sign, and the Greeks seek after wisdom. . . . But God hath chosen the foolish things of the world to confound the wise; and God hath chosen the weak things of the world to confound the things which are mighty" (I Cor. 1:19, 22, 27). In weakness and foolishness this God is met, in the antithesis of reason and power.

The contrast between Hebrew and Greek approaches is considerably overdone, particularly since, as rationalists, we in the name of the Hebrews cut out those facets of their thought which are unreasonable to us. Also, the Greeks knew of the realities beyond reason. There is Socrates with his demon, and Plato, who on occasion could say that living sometimes required of one to dare everything, to defy all shame.[2] And there are in Greek story the ribald Centaurs who clashed with Apollo, and there is Dionysus himself, and there is Aeschylus with his Furies. But it was the charioteer (reason) and Aristotle (with his necessities) and Epictetus (who would cut off noses to enforce reason's dominance) that, by and large, have given us the Greece we choose to remember.

Returning to the survey of the Hebraic-Christian tra-

dition, we recall that it is from Tertullian (*De Carne
Christi*) that the proverb *"credo quia absurdum"* was
derived. Since we have somehow accepted this as a rather
reasonable cliché, it is well to consider it in fuller context
so that, perhaps, we can feel anew the bite of his uncompromising position: "The son of God was crucified: it
does not shame because it is shameful; and the son of
God died; it is absolutely credible because it is absurd;
and having been buried, he rose from the dead; it is certain because it is impossible."

Nor were the Middle Ages without their witnesses to
the call beyond reason. Peter Damian (1007–1072) swept
down on the rationalistic twaddle of his time. For Damian, the devil is the first grammarian who lured Adam
and Eve with the promise of becoming gods, teaching
them the plural declension of this word. In his interpretation of Genesis, ch. 3, Damian interprets the temptation before which Adam and Eve capitulate as the
temptation to rationalism; via his rationalism man
would become God. But Damian's God is beyond the
laws of logic, beyond Aristotle's necessary truths, even
beyond the principle of contradiction, for he is able to
abolish the past.

Like Tertullian's "I believe because it is absurd,"
Luther's reference to the "whore, Reason" has become
easy talk, not heeded, used even in the service of that easy
god kept comfortably in his place as guarantor of my
worth and salvation. Thus we miss the reality that Luther
sought to bring to expression. For Luther, the mystery
was that the *unapproachable* God had approached us;
this unapproachableness was always held in juxtaposition with the approachable, never one without the other.
This God was, in both his unapproachableness and his

approachableness, beyond reason, "beyond tracking out in his mysteries and judgments," absurd in his wrath and his love. This God is most unreasonable.[3] Yet for Luther it is always *this* God who has approached us, again in a totally unreasonable way in the Christ of the cross.[4] The God who comes to us in this fashion is not understood; he is not grasped. He is not even encountered except by that person who has "resigned himself to hell," who has "negated all affirmations." [5]

Blaise Pascal, like Luther and Tertullian, is known primarily by passages that have been quoted beyond hearing: "Not the God of the philosophers, but the God of Abraham and Isaac and Jacob," and "The heart has its reasons which reason cannot know." For Pascal, these are not abstract quotables, but, born out of experience, they are his confessions that meaning is beyond words and reasons. It was out of his own life experiences (a serious illness, a near-fatal accident) that Pascal had branded on his own consciousness the realization that nothingness is not an abstract philosophical impossibility. Because, for him, nothingness was not an abstraction but an experience, the God who is safeguarded by ontological arguments and protected by the principle of noncontradiction is of no consequence—but the God of Abraham and Isaac and Jacob is.

Kierkegaard and the whole theological existentialist tradition that follows him also has rejected the God of the philosophers and gone to the God beyond reason, either to bow before him or to cry horror at his absence. For Kierkegaard, the god of the rationalists, "the god pointed out," is an idol; to seek to point out the God of the Spirit "is to engage in ludicrous twaddle," "to worship under the name of God, a twaddler."

The world built on this twaddler as well as the world constructed on the basis of his absence is, for Dostoevsky, no longer viable. One can find humanness only in the struggle against these encroaching contestants rooted in rationalism:

> But, good Lord, what do I care about the laws of nature and arithmetic if I have my reasons for disliking them, including the one about two and two making four! Of course, I won't be able to breach this wall with my head if I'm not strong enough. But I don't have to accept a stone wall just because it's there and I don't have the strength to breach it.
>
> As if such a wall could really leave me resigned and bring me peace of mind because it's the same as twice two makes four! How stupid can one get? Isn't it much better to recognize the stone walls and the impossibilities for what they are and refuse to accept them if surrendering makes one too sick? [6]

Nor has this call beyond reason come to an end in our own Orwellian twentieth century. There is Rudolf Otto with his "inquiry into the non-rational factor in the idea of the divine"; there is Kafka with his quest through the castle. There is Heidegger, who declares that "to exist" means to be involved without, not contained within, the confines of rational essences. It is in protest against the rationalistic literalization of myth that Bultmann asks after the meaning of myth beyond reasons. Shestov cries out that nothing is necessarily so; that if the truths of reason do not persuade, they thereby lose their status as truths. Wittgenstein, who sometimes seems not to have been completely happy with the nonsense of his favorite Englishman, Lewis Carroll, nonetheless said that his aim was "to teach you to pass from a piece of disguised

nonsense to something that is patent nonsense." [7] Kaz-
antzakis' Zorba tells us that we are always like grocers,
weighing and measuring, calculating our reasons. "Will
no one," he challenges, "ever do anything for the hell of
it?" Zen, proclaiming the irrationality of rationalism,
asks us to hear the sound of one hand clapping. Erich
Fromm speaks of the insanity of our rationalistic consensual validation, and R. D. Laing calls for wholeness
beyond the divided self ruled by the "normal" ego. Jung
sees health in the archetypal pits of the subconscious.
Norman O. Brown tells us that the great world at large
and the intellectual world particularly can find renewed
health only by giving greater attention to Eros and her
dreamers. Ellul calls on us to reject technique with its
rationality and artificiality dominated by the will to
death. Tillich asks us to give up the temptation to a
rationalistic possession of God and wait, if necessary, in
silence. Heschel tells us that God is expressed, not addressed. Sam Keen issues a Dionysian manifesto, and
Harvey Cox calls for a feast of fools. Roszak pleads for
us to be open to the invasion of Centaurs.

This list could go on; it is but a partial overview of
those men who have issued the call to health beyond reason. The call itself is clear; the question to be pursued
now is this: How can we move in this direction?

This putting of the question assumes that there *is*
health beyond reason and that it is possible to move in
this direction. Camus, like so many others, disagreed; he
concluded that the best that one could do is "track down,
illuminate and magnify the human revolt against the irremediable." [8] Perhaps this is so; the revolt possibly is
"against the irremediable." But even if this is so, the
revolt also must be, for the accepted twaddle and insanity
and death is the only alternative. If the abyss cannot be

ignored or skirted or bridged, perhaps we must leap into it, perhaps even affirm it.

Perhaps there is, finally, no God other than the God whom Kafka knew, the God who is absurd, senseless in his justice and senseless in his mercy. But nonetheless the meaning of this world lies with the God who, however much he is in this world, is not simply identical with it. Like Kafka, we may not be sure we can recognize this God, but like Kafka, we must affirm that it is neither healthy nor possible to reject him. We must bow before this God—even in his absurdity. With Amos, we may learn the meaning of ourselves and offer this God due praise even in his condemnation of us.[9]

A theology that grows out of such perspectives can never be very compatible with the prevailing orthodoxies, secular or religious, for it will exist in rejection of their rationalistic bases. Particularly, orthodox Christianity which knows so much about a good and just God with an *ordo salutis* will be repulsed. So also will those recent theological efforts which speak of "recovering the transcendent" or "making room for God" or "letting God be" or "expanding God-consciousness," for such talk, as the grammar itself indicates, knows of a God who, by way of our permission, is allowed to take his place. Yet the fierce wrath and fierce grace of the God of Abraham and Isaac and Jacob will always exert itself, in spite of us; it is never allowed.

This theologizing beyond reason not only will entail a rejection of the rationalistic theologies but will also require the rejection of the identification of theology and doing, activism. The 1960's transformation of Jesus from ascetic to revolutionary activist was predictable but not very helpful. This type of Jesus arrived on the scene just in time to hear Ellul's accurate analysis of the illusion of

politics. This "Jesus the activist" is a good follower in a
dead movement.

The theology beyond rationalism must pursue the dictum that theology is rooted in anthropology. By this I
mean that theology must take as its principal data the dis-
closure of reality which is made manifest in man as he is,
now, concretely. We must seek to come to grips with the
self-understanding and self-confession of individual and
corporate man as he is, now, in our culture, apart from all
sacrosanct reasons. We must go outside and beyond the
wishful thinking of constitutions and programs and declarations and memoranda and creeds. With the artist and
the poet, we must ask how man sees and knows himself
beyond his reasons. That is, we must look beyond the
anthropology of rationalistic dogma into the anthropology of poet and artist and whoever else will seek to see
man as a whole, beyond the necessities of reason.

The problem has not been a crypto-anthropologizing
of theology but rather the rationalism that has dominated our understanding of God and man alike. Our
understanding of man must be rooted in the awareness
that man is more than rational, that man is not simply
reason but is also will and feelings, conscious and subconscious, ego and id. These various, complex factors in
the makeup of man must be given their due. There is not
a charioteer, and there can be none; herein lies the glory
and the mystery and frustration of being human.

This theology must be inclusive rather than exclusive.
It must attempt to undo the fragmentation of man which
is a result of the ascendancy of rationalism with its
money complex and its efficiency of technique. And it
must move beyond our fragmentation into spheres and
nations, religions and beliefs, disciplines and classes, now
and then. It must tour the globe and history, not with

the imperialism of the answerman, but with the openness of the child who has not yet learned how much is
supposed to be foreign to him.

It must be the theology of continual rebirth into continual childlikeness. This rebirth to childlikeness, so un-
intelligible to the rationalistic questions of old Nico-
demus, must be an ongoing process. The child is not, as
some would tell us, the one who will shut up and believe.
Rather, in regaining *die ewige Kinderfrage,* the eternal
question of the child, we will be regaining the "why," the
"for what," which technique with its rationality has lost
for us. By attention to the noises outside the confines of
traditional theology, particularly by attention to the non-
rational, we may at last hear the sound of one hand clapping.

Again, this attention to the non-rational does not mean
anti-rationality. By the non-rational is meant the fearful
and the fascinating which is felt in the contingent and
which obtrudes from the subconscious, which is met by
instinct and intuition. Rudolf Otto in *The Idea of the
Holy,* his classic study of the non-rational, states:

> Not the most concentrated attention can elucidate the ob-
> ject to which it [the experience of the holy] refers, bring-
> ing [it] out of the impenetrable obscurity of feeling into
> the domain of conceptual understanding. It remains
> purely a felt experience, only to be indicated symboli-
> cally by "ideograms." That is what we mean by saying it
> is non-rational.
>
> And the same is true of all the moments of the numin-
> ous experience. The consciousness of a "wholly other"
> evades precise formulation in words and we have to em-
> ploy symbolic phrases which seem sometimes sheer para-
> dox. . . . In ordinary fear and in moral reverence I can
> indicate in conceptual terms what it is that I fear or

revere; injury, e.g., or ruin in the one case, heroism or strength of character in the other. But the object of religious awe or reverence—the *tremendum* and *augustum*, cannot be fully determined conceptually; it is non-rational, as the beauty of a musical composition, which no less eludes complete conceptual analysis.[10]

The experience of the non-rational, as Otto notes, "evades precise formulation," "employs symbolic phrases," "is indicated symbolically." That is, this experience requires and produces the perceptions of the arts and the language of the arts; the theology of the non-rational is closer to poetry than to philosophy.

The perception of the human experience presented to us in the arts includes witness to man's experience of the *mysterium tremendum et fascinans,* the mysterious which is both fearful and fascinating, the ultimate reality beyond reason. Particularly in our time of the dominance of reason, it is in the genre of the grotesque in the arts that we have expressions of the transcendence in our midst which speaks to us beyond our reasons and techniques and death, and offers us hints of the sources of new life, of viable new images, of new perceptions of the ordinary and new possibilities for man. But before we turn to the arts and their use of the grotesque, it is necessary to clarify what is meant by the *mysterium tremendum et fascinans* and to delineate the relation between the grotesque and the holy.

The Numinous

 . . . the *mysterium tremendum et fascinans.*
—Rudolf Otto

In examining the human experience, we encounter not only the rationalistic arguments for and against the existence of God, his attributes, his prerogatives, and the like. Above and beyond reason we encounter also the shadow of that God whom Rudolf Otto described as the *totaliter aliter* (the wholly other) who is known not so much via rational effort as via non-rational experiences which draw man outside and beyond the limits of reason. Borrowing from Otto, I will use his term "numinous" to speak of the holy without reference to its moral or rational aspects. The numinous is felt, not understood; it is expressed, not defined. Otto states: "The truly 'mysterious' object is beyond our apprehension, not only because our knowledge has certain irremovable limits, but because in it we come upon something inherently 'wholly other,' whose kind and character are incommensurable with our own, and before which we therefore recoil in wonder that strikes us chill and numb." [11]

If theology is, in truth, rooted in anthropology, our description of the human situation is incomplete if we chronicle only the arguments that take place within the limits of reason. Theology must speak also of the reality that man experiences beyond these confines; it must speak of the experience of the numinous.

This is the experience of the uncanny, the mysterious, the awful, the majestic, the grotesque. It is the experience beyond rationalizing, subjecting, controlling, or even attributing to a fully definable source. This is the experience of the *mysterium tremendum et fascinans*.

As Otto tells us, this experience of the numinous is of two kinds; it may be both fearful and fascinating, *tremendum et fascinans*. The *tremendum* is the fearful, the non-rational element of awfulness which may be alluded to by terms such as "wrath," "fury," "fire." In speaking of the *tremendum*, Otto even quotes cautiously Boehme's disciple, Johann Pordage, who says, "So I hope then that you will not be angered with me if I impute to God acerbity and bitterness, dread, wrath, fire and the like . . . to express the exalted sensation of God." [12]

The *fascinans* is "the attracting and alluring moment of the numinous," the experience of the marvelous and fascinating which, again, is not reducible to concepts or controls. It includes a Dionysian element which "captivates and transports with a strange ravishment." This *mysterium tremendum et fascinans,* repulsive and attractive, fascinating and frightening, borders the limits of apprehension and comprehension, safely apart from our rationalizations.

Both aspects or functions of the *mysterium* drive home to us that we are not alone; in this experience of irreducible otherness we are before the *totaliter aliter,* the totally other, which moved Augustine to exclaim: "What is that which gleams through me and smites my heart without wounding it? I am both a-shudder and a-glow. A-shudder, in so far as I am unlike it, a-glow in so far as I am like it." [13] And Isaiah could only exclaim: "I am a man of unclean lips."

This *totaliter aliter* doesn't depend on the goodwill of man in order to make itself known. While appreciative of Schleiermacher and his understanding of the "feeling of dependence," one must reject the idea that God is to be inferred as the cause beyond myself which accounts for my feeling of my limits. Rather, this feeling "is itself a first subjective concomitant and effect of another feeling-element which casts it like a shadow but which in itself indubitably has immediate and primary reference to an object outside the self." [14] The "feeling of dependence" is the anthropocentric; the *mysterium* preceded it and allows it, not vice versa.

Also, the *mysterium tremendum et fascinans* must not

and can not be diluted into mere moralisms. The holy is not the good; they are different both in quality and in kind. The diminution of the holy into moral niceness can be supported neither by the origins of the term in the Old Testament nor by the recurrent human experience of the numinous. The god whose holiness is dissolved in goodness is the easy god of rationalistic orthodoxy which goes on to spell out exactly, in its legalistic fashion, of what that goodness consists. He becomes, finally, the easy god from whom I receive a free ticket to heaven in exchange for believing the "right" propositions about Jesus and/or adhering to the "right" moral code.

Further, this *totaliter aliter* is not the passionless God of the rationalists. Divine *apatheia* roots in Aristotle and the Stoics and it has spread throughout much of Christianity, but this is not the living God of anger and love who is attested in the Scriptures and encountered in those events which make up our existence. Sin before the *totaliter aliter* is not a nasty violation of the rules, nor is atonement the good but passionless God's agreement to forget. Otto tells us that "a God who cannot be angry cannot love either; and a God that knows neither love nor anger would be *immobilis* and not the *Deus vivus.*" [15] Rationalistic religion is the dead attempt to schematize the numinous into domesticity.

Ultimately, man's attempt to domesticate the holy has no chance of success. The clash between the numinous and rationalistic religion is not really a contest because God is God, the *totaliter aliter,* beyond reason, while man is but man and cannot contain this God within his concepts. Further, the numinous experience of the reality and otherness of God is the *Seelengrund,* the root experience, of man in the depths of the self, which man himself, *in spite of himself,* attests.

As Otto argues, at the outset of the development of religious consciousness *or in times and places where the genuine expression of the numinous is subjected to the suffocations of rationalism,* the experience of the numinous may take bizarre, even grotesque forms.[16] Perhaps this is simply to say that God is never in danger of capitulating before our attempts to domesticate him; that he does not leave himself without a witness. The reality that man is not alone, in strength or in weakness, is brought home to us in diverse and strange, even bizarre ways.

That the experience of the numinous may be bizarre or even grotesque may seem strange only because it has been bred into us that he is such a nice, easy, comfortable god, lawful and orderly like us, the good bourgeoisie of shop and study. Or perhaps to meet the holy in the grotesque may seem strange to us because we were more comfortable with his absence—"Please, Dad, I'd rather do it myself." But in our extremities, this very strangeness, this grotesqueness, may be our strongest link with the possibility of becoming fully human.

The Numinous, the Arts, and the Grotesque

Art seduces us into the struggle against repression.
                                    —Norman O. Brown

In great art, the point is reached at which we . . . are confronted with the numinous itself, with all its impelling motive power, transcending reason.   —Rudolf Otto

Not infrequently, the rationalist has held the arts suspect. Thus Aristotle in considering Homer says, "The poets lie a great deal." One can suppose that the cause of such petulance may be the poets' refusal to be persuaded

by necessity, by the eternal truths of reason. Likewise
Plato, who identifies the "really real" with the Ideas,
found it necessary to have reservations about art with
its attention to the senses and particulars. For Plato, art
deals only with the shadows and thus is itself a form of
untruth, unlike philosophy and the theoretical sciences.
It would seem that the more the essence of man is located
in reason, the less value is placed on the arts except insofar as they are harnessed to the service of Plato's charioteer.

As I turn now to a very selective examination of the
arts, it is, of course, against the backdrop of the preceding argumentation that man in our time is determined by
technique that is the result of rationalism rooted in our
attraction to and impossible flight from death. The repression of the death instinct takes its revenge; death
dominates our culture, life itself is repressed. There
hangs over us the anxiety of unlived lives; to amend an
ancient rabbinical statement, the judgment *is* the failure
to make use of life.

The psychological reality of repression of the death
instinct, which in the return of the repressed twists into
a flight from life and blind obeisance to death, has its
theological counterpart in our attempts to bring to heel
the numinous, the Unconditional, either by placing it
reasonably and safely beyond the conditional in a spatio-
temporal transcendence, or by some form of attempted
denial of the reality of the human experience of the
numinous. In either of these cases, the numinous lives or
dies by the truths of reason. Francis Schaeffer, whose
Escape from Reason was mentioned earlier as a current
scholarly defense of orthodoxy, no less than Aristotle or
Voltaire or the contemporary man-in-the-street practi-

tioner of atheism, submits the numinous to the eternal
necessities. As Shestov notes, all alike are bound under
Adam's original sin, "that is to say, the knowledge that
what is is necessarily. . . . Quite like the average man,
Aristotle wishes to know nothing of commanding
(*jubere*); he needs only to obey (*parere*) in order to ac-
complish in obeying what he believes, what all men believe, to be the destiny of man. . . . The sources of
jubere are now forever dried up. No one in the world
will ever again command, all will forever obey [cf. the
defenses at the Nuremberg and My Lai trials and the
Watergate hearings]—the great and the small, the right-
eous and sinners, men and gods." [17] And the god obeyed
in our culture is death. That is this generation's thought
of thoughts.

Against this backdrop I wish to argue that in the arts
and, more specifically, in the grotesque in current art, we
find a multifaceted rejection of rationalism and repression and the dominance of death. In the artistic expression of the grotesque we find a call to hope and health
as man is presented *sub specie mysterium tremendum et
fascinans,* as a being caught up under the fearful and
fascinating experience of the numinous, beyond all that
is necessarily so.

Perhaps Freud is only half right in arguing that the
function of art is to regain the lost laughter of infancy.
Perhaps the function of art is to move us not only beyond
repression but also beyond dualism to an affirmation of
the dialectic of life and death. Theologically speaking,
this movement is a possibility not because one wishes it
but because, overruling the lawful and orderly god of
orthodoxy, its kin and its black sheep, there is the passionate God of fire and dance who encounters us still, in

spite of ourselves, in the experience of the *mysterium tremendum et fascinans*. It is this God who is attested and who is addressed to us in our extremities via the grotesque in the arts.

A scanning of any good library in the arts or humanities confirms the current interest in the grotesque. As both Arthur Clayborough and Wolfgang Kayser have made indelibly clear in their recent, thorough studies of the grotesque, during no period in history has this genre been so plentiful or so powerful in arts and literature as during the past century.

There have been several critical dissertations, books and articles on this subject in recent years, but they have focused primarily on the history of the grotesque and on the aesthetic; there has been very little concern for the relation of the grotesque and psychoanalytical or theological questions. However, these works have been helpful in clarifying the origins and development of the grotesque and have emphasized and made known the prominence of the grotesque in contemporary arts.[18]

The beginning of the term "grotesque" is generally traced back to the Rome of Nero and Titus, where there developed a peculiar style of decoration used in the chambers (*grotte*) of several buildings. The murals decorating these *grotte* included fantastic, bizarre interminglings of plants and animals and people.[19] Knowledge of these *grotte* was lost for several centuries until they were excavated about 1500 and their artistic style came to be much imitated. Thus, for example, Cardinal Piccolomini instructed the artist Pinturicchio (ca. 1502) to decorate the ceiling vaults of the library of the Cathedral of Siena "in the grotesque fashion." [20] This is the origin of our word "grotesque," but not, of course, the origin of art of the grotesque mode, as any examination of ancient or primitive art shows. Further, the term itself may be traced back behind Italian and Latin to the Greek, *kruptē* ("pit," "vault") and *kruptein* ("to hide," "to make secret," "to conceal"), terms of interest because of their psychological overtones.

Gradually in the period after the sixteenth century, following the development of the imitative art style, the term is taken over into a more general usage and according to Arthur Clayborough in his excellent study, *The Grotesque in English Literature,*

> becomes applicable to whatever is incongruous with the accepted norm, in life or art. In ordinary colloquial use it is commonly associated as a pejorative with the unintentionally ridiculous or the monstrous. In critical use, it may be employed to describe any style of art which deviates from conventional patterns. . . . The primary sense in both these extended uses of the word, whether as noun or adjective, is that of incongruity with the real or normal.[21]

In order to clarify further the grotesque, Clayborough delineates four types of definitions common among writers of the past three centuries:

1. A definition based on the attitudes of the artist, his intentions and reactions; i.e., a definition in terms of *Schaffensvorgang,* or creative impetus.
2. A definition focussed on the effects or impressions created on the reader or audience.
3. A definition attempted via relationship with similar categories such as the sublime, the ugly, the fantastic, the comic, et cetera.
4. A definition based on the characteristic features of a limited but representative group of works.[22]

As I use the term "grotesque," I mean that which is incongruous with the accepted norms, that which by way of its ability to frighten or fascinate violates the standards, cultural and artistic, which consensual validation has sanctified. The reality of the grotesque in both art and life may be experienced as negative or positive, depending on one's viewpoint. However, the term should certainly not be pejorative in and of itself. While I do not find Clayborough's third suggestion very helpful, I feel that it is necessary to intermingle the other three approaches, even though this may create a certain lack of precision.

Thus as I move into the examination of certain works that contain features which allow them to be called grotesque (i.e., incongruous with accepted norms), I am concerned to keep in mind the creator's intentions, insofar as these are accessible, and also the effect these works seem to have on their audiences.[23]

I have chosen to focus on the grotesque for two basic, interrelated reasons. First, the grotesque is peculiarly prominent in the art and literature of our time. That is, this mode of expression is very common in the contemporary arts as their creators seek to confront us with their understanding of the nature of man in the twentieth century. If for no other reason, theology which grows out of anthropology must concern itself with the grotesque in our time because of the prominence and pervasiveness of this genre in contemporary depictions of man.

Second, if one feels the importance of the non-rational in theology and believes, with Otto, that the grotesque may be a basic mode of response to the human experience of the numinous with its fearful and fascinating aspects, then one is predisposed to a theological consideration of the grotesque, for one will suspect that the grotesque in arts and literature has something to say to a theology in the extremities of rationalism.

For these reasons (because it is very prominent in contemporary culture and because the grotesque may speak to us of the reality of the holy beyond the limits of reason) let us proceed with a selective examination of the grotesque. From these perspectives, let us consider in some detail as contemporary examples of artists of the grotesque some facets of the work of the writer Flannery O'Connor; the film makers Buñuel and Fellini; the artist Picasso; and the playwright Ionesco. Along with these more detailed considerations, let us briefly scan other artists and movements, noting the prominence and pervasiveness of the grotesque and suggesting possibilities for the interpretation of this phenomenon.

4

The Grotesque in Fiction:
Flannery O'Connor

God's material form is necessarily grotesque.
—Christian Morgenstern

In this chapter and the two that follow, it is argued that
the grotesque in contemporary art entails a multifaceted
rejection of rationalism and technology and the dominance of death. In the artistic expression of the grotesque,
we find a call to hope and health as man is presented *sub
specie mysterium tremendum et fascinans,* beyond all
that is necessarily so. It is contended that as we examine
this prominent, recurrent expression of the grotesque
in the perceptions of man presented by these artists, we
find a powerful testimony to the reality of the holy as it
is experienced in non-rational ways which are ultimately
beyond our analyzing and managing. And we find also
new images of hope beyond our rationalistic dead ends.

Flannery O'Connor

> The dragon is by the side of the road, watching those who pass. Beware lest he devour you. We go to the father of souls, but it is necessary to pass by the dragon.
> —St. Cyril of Jerusalem

> Warn the children of God of the terrible speed of mercy.
> —Flannery O'Connor, from
> *The Violent Bear It Away*

An exceptionally large number of significant contemporary writers work with the genre of the grotesque. A partial listing includes such artists as Friedrich Dürrenmatt, Franz Kafka, Christian Morgenstern, Katherine Anne Porter, Thomas Mann, Eudora Welty, Carson McCullers, William Faulkner, Tolkien, John Steinbeck, and many others. A survey of the work of these authors is beyond the scope of this study. I have had to be selective and have chosen, therefore, as a representative writer who works in and through the grotesque, Flannery O'Connor.

O'Connor is one of the ablest American writers of this century, and she uses the grotesque with singular effect as a means of protest against the submission to reason and technology and death which dominate our time. Also, she consciously and explicitly attests the experience of the numinous, the encounter with the holy beyond reason by which man is released from the life he would manage on his own terms and is embraced with the freedom to be himself, in spite of all. Her characters, like Job, cannot escape their hard master who grotesquely drives them beyond reason. Still, they also, like Job, maintain their own ways before Him.

This is not an attempt to survey O'Connor's life and

Weltanschauung, nor is it a detailed analysis of all her fiction.[1] The concern is simply to examine aspects of her fiction in the light of the preceding discussion and under the umbra of the *mysterium* and the grotesque.

A native of Milledgeville, Georgia, immersed in a Catholic sacramental view of life in which, as Otto noted, "the numinous is to be found as a living factor of singular power," this champion of St. Cyril's dragon created during the few years of her active literary life two novels and a couple dozen short stories which are, through their use of the grotesque, a concentrated call to her contemporaries to a God beyond managing in a life beyond reason.

O'Connor's work is consciously grotesque according to the intentions of the author and, as the diverse critical responses verify, it is experienced as grotesque by her readers as well. Her use of this mode of expression is rooted in her understanding of our culture and its malaise. For O'Connor, our times are marked above all by our lack of awareness of St. Cyril's dragon: "Since the eighteenth century, the popular spirit of each succeeding age has tended more and more to the view that the ills and mysteries of life will eventually fall before the scientific advances of man, a belief that is still going strong even though this is the first generation to face total extinction because of these advances."[2] In comparison with the statements she makes through her characters and their torturous adventures, this is certainly one of her mildest statements concerning what she sees to be the dominant problem of our culture.

For O'Connor, any literature that merely mirrors our society is aiding and abetting a view of life which is, for her, unreal and deadly. Rather, life is not what it seems on the surface and the artist should make this known:

> Life is and will remain essentially mysterious. . . . What the writer sees on the surface will be of interest to him only as he can go through it into an experience of mystery itself. His kind of fiction will always be pushing its own limits outward toward the limits of mystery because . . . the meaning of a story does not begin except at a depth where adequate motivation and adequate psychology and the various determinations have been exhausted. He will be interested in possibility rather than probability . . . characters forced out to meet evil and grace and who act on a trust beyond themselves—whether they know very clearly what it is they act upon or not. To the modern mind, this kind of character and his creator are typical Don Quixotes, tilting at what is not there.[3]

O'Connor uses the grotesque because of what she perceives to be the deafness of modern man to his own predicament: "To the hard of hearing you shout; to the almost blind you draw large and startling figures." Further, like Thomas Mann and many others before her, she believed that "certain attainments of the soul and the intellect are impossible without disease, without insanity, without spiritual crimes." [4]

For these reasons, she peoples her works with grotesques, physical and spiritual, secular and religious. There is Hulga-Joy with her artificial leg in "Good Country People"; there is hyper-tatooed Obadiah Elihue Parker of "Parker's Back"; and there is club-footed Rufus Johnson in "The Lame Shall Enter First." There is the hermaphrodite of "Temple of the Holy Ghost" and the imbecilic Enoch Emery of *Wise Blood*. There are the spiritual grotesques like old Mason Tarwater and his nephew in *The Violent Bear It Away*, and there is Haze Motes and Solace Layfield in *Wise Blood*. And there are secular grotesques such as the robotlike Sheppard of

"The Lame Shall Enter First" and the unforgettable non-character, Rayber, of *The Violent Bear It Away* and the sort-of-intellectuals (all O'Connor's intellectuals must be qualified thus; it is part of her call to a truer wisdom), Julian of "Everything That Rises Must Converge" and Asbury of "The Enduring Chill."

The world of these grotesques is a world of strange and eerie and sudden violence: The Misfit and his cronies murder the vacationing family in "A Good Man Is Hard to Find"; Haze makes The Prophet strip and then runs his old Essex back and forth over him; the boys burn the Cope place in "A Circle in the Fire"; ugly Mary Grace clobbers Mrs. Turpin in "Revelation"; Fortune beats his favorite granddaughter to death in "A View of the Woods."

The list goes on. O'Connor's people look grotesque on the outside and they look grotesque on the inside and they do grotesque things. All her characters are "displaced persons," not just the characters in the story by that name. This is so because the world itself is out of joint and the only way to address us in our extremities is through the blatantly grotesque in the hopes that this will make visible the hidden grotesqueness of our chrome-plated fences around the dragon. In an essay on the grotesque in fiction, O'Connor says: "In these grotesque works we find that the writer has made alive some experience which we are not accustomed to observe every day or which the ordinary man may never experience in his ordinary life. . . . There are strange skips and gaps, . . . yet the characters have an inner coherence as they lean away from typical patterns toward mystery and the unexpected." [5]

Within the grotesque, O'Connor articulates what she

sees as the only hope for health in a world she sees as sick, perhaps even too sick to hear this strange voice: "Thomas Mann has said that the grotesque is the true antibourgeois style, but I believe that in this century, the general reader has managed to connect the grotesque with the sentimental, for whenever he speaks of it favorably, he seems to associate it with the writer's compassion." [6]

As one looks more deeply into that which O'Connor believes constitutes the crises of our time, one sees that for her the overwhelming factor is our technological rationalism. This is shown most powerfully through Rayber, one of the three main characters in *The Violent Bear It Away*. Rayber is the schoolteacher uncle of Tarwater, the snotty-nosed belligerent who is the protagonist of this novel. Rayber sets for himself the task of freeing the boy from the God-drenched past he has known under the tutelage of old Mason Tarwater, the recently deceased, hoary, violent, half-mad prophet-moonshiner who wills not only, like Camus's humanist, to tell men that they are not God, but also to tell them that God is, and that he is inexorably and inevitably upon them.

O'Connor's description of Rayber is her classic description of that age which has flowered out of the eighteenth century "Enlightenment." Rayber is, almost literally, a mechanical man with "two small drill-like eyes" which, peering intently out from behind his black-rimmed glasses, seem to bore out from his own soullessness as if to capture the souls of others. (He had made such an attempt on the old man by trying to capture him in an article on his neuroses which was printed "in a schoolteacher magazine.") These eyes of Rayber look like "something human trapped in a switch box." He wears an electrical hearing aid, a device referred to as "the ma-

chine," "a metal box . . . joined by a cord to a plug in
his ear," prompting Tarwater to wonder if "his head
ran by electricity," so that he asks the teacher if his head
lights up.

The old man has told Tarwater that Rayber lives
"with his guts in his head," and warned him that

> if you were to go there, the first thing he would do would
> be to test your head and tell you what you were thinking
> and how come you were thinking it and what you ought
> to be thinking instead. And before long you wouldn't
> belong to yourself no more you would belong to him.

Following the old man's death, young Tarwater nonetheless goes into the city, to Rayber, supposedly to exalt
in his own freedom but also driven by his own mad pro-
phetic compulsions, including the compulsion to baptize Rayber's idiot child, Bishop. There he finally acts
out this compulsion in his drowning-baptizing of Bishop.
Rayber, who had previously attempted to rid himself of
this child but was prevented from doing so, not only by
his own inability to act (instead of think) but also by
his "morbid" clinging, embarrassing love for the child,
stands looking out of a window down at this happening
in the lake before him, his heart beating "with a dull
mechanical beat."

> He stood waiting for the raging pain, the intolerable
> hurt that was his due, to begin, so that he could ignore
> it, but he continued to feel nothing. He stood light-
> headed at the window and it was not until he realized
> there would be no pain that he collapsed.

The control that Rayber has gained is the control of the
technician over the robot. "Do you think in the box . . .
or do you think in your head?" asks Tarwater. For

O'Connor, Rayber embodies the rationalist's position, a position as untenable as it is ineffectual. For her, Tarwater's opinion on airplanes is the fitting epitaph for the technological, rationalistic society and its pride of accomplishment: "I wouldn't give nothing for no airplane. A buzzard can fly."

It is not only the secular rationalist like Rayber but also the representatives of orthodoxy with their pleasant management religion who are lampooned by O'Connor. An insight into her evaluation of this religion is given in a personal letter: "I would like to go to California for about two minutes to further these researches . . . into the ways of the vulgar. Did you see the picture of Roy Rogers' horse attending a church service in Pasadena?" [7]

Particularly Haze Motes of *Wise Blood* with his attempt to found "The Holy Church Without Christ" is the counterpoint against which O'Connor plays out her portrayal of the easy religion and its easy god. One of his antagonists, Onnie Jay Holy, alias Hoover Shoates, indicates the underlying characteristic of this acculturated religion when he says:

> "Now I just want to give you folks a few reasons why you can trust this church. . . . In the first place, friends, you can rely on it that it's nothing foreign connected with it. You don't have to believe nothing you don't understand and approve of. If you don't understand it, it ain't true, and that's all there is to it. No jokers in the deck, friends. . . .
>
> "Now, friends, . . . I want to tell you a second reason why you can absolutely trust this church—it's based on the Bible. Yes sir! It's based on your own personal interpitation of the Bible, friends. You can sit at home and interpit your own Bible however you feel in your heart it ought to be interpited. That's right, . . . just the way

Jesus would have done it. Gee, I wisht I had my gittarr here."

A culture religion with a new jesus to suit every possible whim, safely based on the Bible which means exactly what you want it to mean, guaranteed understandable on your own terms—this is a religion that will sell.[8]

A more orthodox version of religion than that of Hoover Shoates is broadsided via the character of Mrs. Turpin in the finely-honed little story "Revelation." Mrs. Turpin's whole world is fraught with a Jesus who might have made her white trash or nigger or ugly, but had the good sense to make her the nice, clean, comfortable, hard-working, respectable bigot she is. Self-assured, she wails out,

> "When I looked up and He looked down,
>   And wona these days I know I'll we-eara crown."

God's in his place and he knows exactly what that is; therefore, all is right in Mrs. Turpin's world.

Into this artificial world, as disquieting and monstrous in its own way as the brace shop in "The Lame Shall Enter First," there cuts the violence of grace, grace like cold steel, grace which is met first of all in the wrath that tears man loose from his reasons. Mrs. Turpin encounters this grace through the wrathful ministrations of Mary Grace, the ugly and rebellious college girl who, not able to stand Mrs. Turpin's self-righteous prattling in the doctor's office, explodes, calling her "a wart hog from hell," and pastes her in the side of the head with a book. This painful clash is the beginning of the transformation of Mrs. Turpin.

Another example of the recurrent, harsh grotesqueness of grace in O'Connor's work is found in "A Good Man

Is Hard to Find." This is the story of a family of five that is headed through Georgia to a vacation in Florida. There is Bailey, the empty young father, his even more nondescript wife, their cantankerous children, John Wesley and June Star, and Bailey's mother—all militantly vapid and philistine. "Grandmother especially displays a soul so empty that it seems to reverberate with the echoes of her own incessant and aimless chatter." [9] Her solitary topics are her intimations of past splendors and her suggestions of what might have been.

After a stop for some of Red Sammy's barbecue, they continue on while Grandma plays out a tale about an old plantation and secret panels and hidden treasure which she knows are just off the highway. Bailey finally relents: "All right, but get this: this is the only time we're going to stop for anything like this. This is the one and only time."

Going down the dirt road to which Grandma has directed them, Grandma, anxious over her uncertain directions, upsets the basket in which she had hidden away her cat. The cat jumps on Bailey, he panics, and the car ends upside down in a gulch off the side of the road. The accident delights the children, even though no one is killed, and convinces Grandma she hadn't better mention that she remembered the plantation was in Tennessee.

At this point another car happens on the scene, bringing with it a fat boy, a man in khaki pants and

an older man than the other two. His hair was just beginning to gray and he wore silver-rimmed spectacles that gave him a scholarly look. He had a long creased face and didn't have on any shirt or undershirt. He had on blue jeans that were too tight for him and was holding a black hat and a gun. The two boys also had guns.

Grandma soon recognizes the older man as The Misfit, an escaped psychopath whose picture was in the morning paper. The Misfit allows that it might have been better for all of them if she "hadn't of reckernized" him. Grandma accelerates her endless stream of banalities: "You wouldn't shoot a lady, would you?" "I know you're a good man. You don't look a bit like you have common blood. I know you must come from nice people!" She cries, "Pray, pray" as their plight becomes totally obvious when Bailey and the boy are taken off to be shot. "I know you come from nice people! Pray! Jesus, you ought not to shoot a lady. I'll give you all the money I've got!"

> There were two more pistol reports and the grandmother raised her head like a parched old turkey hen crying for water and called, "Bailey Boy, Bailey Boy!" as if her heart would break. . . .
>
> . . . She saw the man's face twisted close to her own as if he were going to cry and she murmured, "Why you're one of my babies. You're one of my own children!" She reached out and touched him on the shoulder. The Misfit sprang back as if a snake had bitten him and shot her three times through the chest. Then he put his gun down on the ground and took off his glasses and began to clean them.

Grandma used up all the coins with which she had come to barter—the mask of the lady, the sympathetic understanding, prayer and money. At each attempt she is turned back by The Misfit: "Nome, I ain't a good man." "Nome. It wasn't no mistake [in reference to his having been sentenced to prison]. They had the papers on me." "Nobody had nothing I wanted," he tells her when she suggests he commits his crimes in order to obtain things he had been deprived of.

The Misfit's references to Jesus draw out the nature of his character even more clearly. He says:

> "Jesus thrown everything off balance. It was the same case with Him as with me except He hadn't committed any crime and they could prove I had committed one. . . ."

> "Jesus was the only One that ever raised the dead . . . and He shouldn't have done it. He thrown everything off balance. If He did what He said, then it's nothing for you to do but throw away everything and follow Him, and if He didn't, then it's nothing for you to do but enjoy the few minutes you got left the best way you can—by killing somebody or burning down his house or doing some other meanness to him. No pleasure but meanness."

But then in the final exchange with which the story closes, when the fat boy, Bobby Lee, says, " 'Some fun!' " The Misfit responds: " 'Shut up, Bobby Lee. It's no real pleasure in life.' "

As strange and harsh as "A Good Man Is Hard to Find" may seem, it is not an atypical O'Connor story; in fact, a criticism of her work is its striking sameness. It is because of material like this that she has been accused by some critics of being on the devil's side, intermingling a complex disbelief in the holy with attraction to it. However, it is precisely because of material like this that she is so significant theologically.

"To society, the Misfit is a psychopathic killer; to Flannery O'Connor, he would seem to be a kind of saint manqué, cutting through the cliché-ridden, heedless lives of the people he murders to radical questions of depth of spirit, of the reality of good and evil." [10] For O'Connor, The Misfit is the dragon by whom we must pass or through whose jaws we must go if there is to be any restoration of health, beyond the Raybers and the Sheppards and the Copes and the Hopewells who are the mark of our time. When one grasps, or is grasped by, the experience which Haze Motes articulates in these words, "Where you come from is gone, where you thought you were going to never was there, and where you are is no good unless you can get away from it," then those empty reasons out of which we try to live are exposed, swept away, and we are left with nothing. But for O'Connor, this is a holy Nothingness which alone can refine us, can, in our current cultural malaise, clear away our artificial and invalid attempts at security such as our rationalistic, technological "achievements" or our rationalistic, managed religion. For O'Connor, Nothingness is not a manageable abstraction like Parmenides' non-being but is the dragon himself—and there is no other path to life than that which he commands.

For O'Connor, sin is not our violation of moralisms, petty or otherwise. For her, as for Shestov, sin is the living out of that knowledge of good and evil, founded in our rationalism, issuing in people with their guts in their heads. Such people can live complacently with the self-righteousness of Mrs. Turpin or with the blindness and emptiness of Rayber.

Against the gods of such people, Luther poses the God "beyond tracking out in his mysteries and his fearful marvels and his incomprehensible judgments," who is in his essence hidden away from all reason, knows no measure, law or aim, and is verified in the paradox.[11] Luther even ventures to designate this awe-inspiring, non-rational character of the deity as *"Deus ipse, ut est in sua natura et maiestate,"* God as he really is in his own nature and majesty.[12] We tend to back away from the implications of this dangerous, uncontrollable God who might tear us out of our comforts—but need we reconsider just what these comforts are or the price we have paid for them and forced on others?

This unreasonable God claims us totally, in his own time, in his own way, as he claimed Haze Motes and Tarwater and Obadiah Elihue Parker and Abraham and Isaac and Jacob. For O'Connor, the human response—the only human response and the only response that could claim to be fully human—to the experience of the *mysterium* is a response of total, consuming commitment, now, in this place. Thus she seeks—or sees—the interrelation of the reversal of our rationalism and the healing of our fragmentation. It is Tarwater who can do, while Rayber, with his guts in his head, is the paralyzed spectator. Also she knows that in this experience itself there is resolved the dialectic of the Unconditional and the conditional in the unconditional sanctification of all that is. This hope Miss O'Connor summarizes powerfully, beautifully, in Mrs. Turpin's vision as she stands at the hog pen watching Claude's pickup drive off, watching the sunset:

> She saw . . . a vast swinging bridge extending upward from the earth through a field of living fire. Upon it a vast horde of souls were rumbling toward heaven. There were whole companies of white-trash, clean for the first time in their lives, and bands of black niggers in white robes, and battalions of freaks and lunatics shouting and clapping and leaping like frogs. And bringing up the end of the procession was a tribe of people whom she recognized at once as those who, like herself and Claude, had always had a little of everything and the God-given wit to use it right. She leaned forward to observe them closer.

They were marching behind the others with great dignity, accountable as they had always been for good order and common sense and respectable behavior. They alone were on key. Yet she could see by their shocked and altered faces that even their virtues were being burned away. She lowered her hands and gripped the rail of the hog pen.

For Miss O'Connor, the word that, because of reason's advance, we face total extinction is not the last word. Rather, if we can recognize the freak in ourselves, we perhaps still have some possibility of being made whole men. The experience of the *mysterium tremendum et fascinans* leads one, ultimately, to risk the hope that everything that rises must converge.[13]

5

The Grotesque in Film: Buñuel and Fellini

It is . . . [through] the seeing man that we are contemplating the true nature of grotesqueness.　　—Ruskin

Before Plato with his charioteer and Aristotle with his necessary truths deemed otherwise, the wise man was not the man of pure intellect, the rationalistic philosopher or scientist, but the sage who carried in his visions the secrets of the past and the hopes of the future. He might be seer or prophet or diviner, but always he was looked on as the man who could see deeper, farther, more than other men. Thus the Greek word for "I know" is *oida*, the perfect tense of the verb "to see," which once meant simply "I have seen." Obviously the ancient Greek did not think that all visual experiences, per se, brought wisdom or spiritual insight. However, as he indicated linguistically, authentic knowing goes beyond the simple cognitive processes and involves the accomplished experiences of the whole person. During most of the history of our race, the wise man was not the man who captured thought via reason and concept but the visionary, the man who had seen.

John Ruskin with his distinction between creating and seeing tells us that "the greatest thing a human soul ever does in this world is to see something, and tell what it saw in a plain way. Hundreds of people can talk for one who can think but thousands can think for one who can see. To see clearly is poetry, prophecy and religion, all in one."

Further, in his early analysis of the grotesque, Ruskin tells us that it is the seeing man who will explore with us and for us "the true nature of grotesqueness," both the "sportive grotesque" and the "terrible," the two major subtypes according to his classifications.

Thus it is with considerable justification that we look, however briefly, at the contemporary cinema, that most powerful art of the seeing man, for some of the most terrifying and fascinating considerations of the grotesque in our time. One might, with profit, carry out a lengthy study of the grotesque in cinema; however, at this point it is necessary to limit our considerations. For our purposes, I have chosen examples primarily from the works of Buñuel and Fellini.

Luis Buñuel

"un desperé, un passioné appel au meutre."
—Buñuel, concerning *L'Age d'Or*

If we approach the materials by way of Ruskin's distinction between the sportive and terrible grotesque, the master of the terrible grotesque in cinema who is particularly deserving of consideration is Luis Buñuel.

Why Buñuel's work might be included in a considera-

tion of contemporary grotesques is obvious: in his films
we find scenes depicting a dog squashed, a son killed
wantonly by his father, a Duc de Blangis Christ, an orgy-
parody of da Vinci's *Last Supper* enacted to the strains of
Hallelujah Chorus, et cetera. The question is this: What,
if any, is the significance of the supreme grotesque artis-
try of this brilliant and throughgoing atheist in this consideration of the relation to the grotesque and the *mysterium tremendum et fascinans*? Of what theological significance might Buñuel's work be?

Buñuel was born into a well-to-do landed Spanish family in 1900. Studious in his youth, he was educated in a
Jesuit secondary school which was to become one of the
prime sources of his enduring revolt against religion. He
objected particularly to the diversion of sexual energies
to the love—even physical love—of the Virgin. While
Buñuel's instinctual and acute revolt against the religion
that he encountered and perceived remains a vital and
meaningful motif throughout his work, one could appreciate more evidence of a wider awareness of the varieties
of theology, particularly the theology of the past several
decades.

In a student residence in Madrid, he became part of an
illustrious group that included Dali, Ortega y Gasset, and
García Lorca. In 1925, Buñuel went to Paris, seemingly
with the intent of learning cinema. After an appren-
ticeship under Jean Epstein, he made, in 1928 in cooperation with Dali, his first film, the frequently shown
Un Chien Andalou. The separations and evaluations of
the respective contributions of Buñuel and Dali in the
making of this film vary widely. Ado Kyrou, a Buñuel
biographer, states that "Buñuel sought to catch a glimpse
of that incandescent world in which dream and reality

mingle in a magnificent gesture of liberation; Dali hoped to shock the bourgeoisie." [1] Though neither man was as yet directly involved in surrealism, this film was much acclaimed by the surrealists as "a doctrinaire expression of automatism," and Buñuel and Dali were swept into the movement.[2]

Buñuel's second film, *L'Age d'Or* (1930), also was supposedly made in cooperation with Dali; however, Dali's contribution seems minimal. Rather, the film serves as a program piece which Buñuel's later work serves to explicate. Therefore, a concise summarization of its contents is a worthwhile foundation for our consideration of Buñuel's masterpiece, *Viridiana,* and its grotesques.

The film begins as a documentary about scorpions (insects as the monsters, the grotesques that may inhabit the planet as man in his self-destruction vacates it, have always interested Buñuel), but abruptly shifts from such factuality to a scene of bishops celebrating mass in a landscape crowded with huge rocks (a subtitle has noted: "The scorpion belongs to that branch of the spider family that generally lives under stones"). In the same area as the mass, the inhabitants of the country, the shabby and grotesque survivors of a dying age, battle the mysterious Majorcans for whom the bishops are an advance guard. The inhabitants defeated, the bishops move through the rocks to the spot where they will lay the foundations for the new Rome. At this point, they are interrupted by "a man and a woman in a fiercely lascivious embrace, rolling in the mud."

> This is *amour fou,* a completely single-minded, unquestioning passion which disregards circumstances, annihilates time and place, and is for Buñuel the strongest, most explosive force in the world, or at least can be if it is

accepted without question or doubt or hesitation or qual-
ification. The lovers (Gaston Modot and Lya Lys) are
separated like animals and Rome is built on their separation (the Church, that is, is the great perverter of humanity, the great frustrating agent in human life).[3]

This love scene sets the stage for the remainder of the
film. Society—its laws, its religions, its inhibitions—seeks
to rip the lovers apart, but this proves impossible on
both a physical and a psychic level.

The film ends with scenes of the Château de Selligny,
where de Sade's survivors from the one hundred and
twenty days of sodomy totter out, exhausted, disheveled,
disguised as a variety of characters. Christ is played by
the Duc de Blangis himself. A last-surviving victim appears and the Christ-figure count kills her. The film ends
with a shot of "a snow-covered cross, laced with women's
hair, whipped by the wind and whitened by the snow."

Viridiana (1961) is, I believe, Buñuel's masterpiece
par excellence, the fullest, most poetic statement of his
views to date; also, this film contains some of Buñuel's
harshest grotesques. Statements by Buñuel's biographers
to the effect that *L'Age d'Or* involves frenzied anticleri-
calism, while *Viridiana* works out of a peaceful atheism
seem inconsequential, for the force of the statement certainly is unchanged. The consistency of Buñuel's work is
formidable; it is, throughout, *"un desperé, un passioné
appel au meutre,"* a desperate, passionate call to murder.

Viridiana is the name of a young girl, a novice who is
about to take her final vows for entrance into the convent.
The mother superior urges her to make a visit to her uncle, her only relative, before doing so; reluctantly Viridiana agrees. She goes to the estate of this wealthy uncle,
Don Jaime, whom she does not know well, and there she

seems to enjoy the naturalness of the country life—gathering eggs, milking cows. But there are already disquieting motifs established in phallic symbols such as the teat of the cow from which she withdraws her hand and the handles of the jump rope used by Rita, the daughter of the housekeeper, Ramona.

The shadowy discomfort felt about the uncle begins to take shape. We learn that his wife died of a heart attack on their wedding night before the marriage was consummated. Don Jaime has, in a fashion, respected the marriage laws and is left with a twisted sexuality despite an excursion that brought him a bastard son. Nightly, Don Jaime dresses in his dead wife's wedding regalia. Further, he is captivated by the similarity between his wife and his niece—he must have her. When she rebuffs his honorable approach in shock, he drugs her, takes her to his room, and stops only just short of raping the corpse-like body on the bed.

The next day, in an attempt to force her to stay with him instead of return to the convent he tells Viridiana he has violated her, that she cannot any longer take her vows. Then he confesses he hasn't. Viridiana is about to leave via a bus from the local village when the police stop her; Don Jaime has hung himself, using the jump rope.

Knowing her role in this death, Viridiana feels that she must leave the conventional religious role and make amends on her own. She and Don Jaime's illegitimate son, Jorge, inherit the estate. While he turns his effort toward modernizing and working the estate, she collects a motley, truly grotesque crew of beggars—lame, blind, halt, leprous—gives them food and shelter, and seeks to move them toward the holy life.

One day when Jorge and Viridiana must go into town on business, the riffraff break into the great house and expropriate it for the most devastating orgy-parody on film. The climax comes when scruffy Enedina asks them to pose for a picture that she will take with an old camera her parents gave her. As the grotesques arrange themselves à la da Vinci's *Last Supper* with the blind man, the one person in the film portrayed as truly evil, taking his place as Christ,

> Enedina, a ragged old hag, sweeps her very ample skirt up to her face. The photograph is taken. She chokes with laughter behind her skirt. They all relax their poses and break out into disordered babbling. The group comes to life again and the hubbub reigns supreme.
>
> The leper now appears lecherous and gay. He goes up to the phonograph, takes a record, puts it down dissatisfied, and then picks up another at random. He puts it on the record player. It is the Hallelujah Chorus from Handel's *Messiah*. He plays it very loud and this seems to give him pleasure and even more strength. He glides toward Don Jaime's room. Before going in, he looks at them defiantly but they don't seem to notice. . . .
>
> . . . In the middle of the hubbub the leper appears at the door of Don Jaime's room in Doña Elvira's wedding veil and corset. He begins to dance to the music of the Hallelujah Chorus. It is a wild grotesque dance.[4]

The others join in, gyrating, copulating in their bizarre pageant.

Jorge and Viridiana arrive unexpectedly. Most of the beggars leave, but the blind man and the leper subdue Jorge, and the blind man, wearing the jump rope as a belt, sets about raping Viridiana, whose hands tighten about the handles of the rope. At the last moment, Jorge bribes the leper into clubbing the blind man with a shovel; the police arrive, the scene ends.

The film closes with Viridiana coming cautiously into the room where Jorge is playing cards with the housekeeper (with whom he has formed a liaison). Viridiana accepts Jorge's invitation to join them: "She has come over to his side, the side of practical full-blooded materialism which sees that things get done while religion falls back on aimless ritual and denies the body its due." [5] The film, which had started with Handel's Hallelujah Chorus, closes with the frenzied rhythms of early rock.

Buñuel voices his "desperate, passionate call for murder" against *all* the prevailing orthodoxies: "I am against conventional morality, traditional sacred cows, sentimentality and all that moral filth of society which comes into it." [6] Buñuel is against these things because he feels they are the means by which the establishment maintains its stranglehold throughout Western culture. For him, the conventional morality is the true immorality, the sanctified understructure of what Buñuel has referred to as our most unjust social institutions such as religion, fatherland, family, culture—everything that people call the pillars of society.

The conventional morality is the sanctification of death, the death that Don Jaime lives for in the decades after his wife's death, the death from which Viridiana narrowly escapes, the death of the self-imprisoned sophisticates of Buñuel's later film, *The Exterminating Angel*, the death the Majorcans bring and the bishops bless in *L'Age d'Or*.

A most perceptive insight into Buñuel's understanding of good and evil, of morality and immorality, is given by Ado Kyrou in his study of Buñuel:

Note that when in a Buñuel film we meet "good" (Viridiana, for example) or "evil" (her protégés) this does not mean what it means in the films of other people because for Buñuel absolute good and absolute evil are beguiling, impassioning monstrosities. Buñuel loves Viridiana the pure as well as her impure wards.[7]

Death, the death to fight, according to Buñuel is the death of the unlived life. Don Jaime is dead, the leper of the macabre dance is alive; Jorge is almost alive, Viridiana is very nearly dead; the Majorcans and their bishops are dead, the two lovers are alive. The death of the unlived life is the final accomplishment of Western culture; the only true sanity and the only real morality is to revolt against this death.

Concerning Christianity, Buñuel argues passionately and convincingly that it is the cornerstone of the morality of the unlived life; this is symbolized in *Viridiana* by such things as the little cross which, on pressing a button, becomes a nasty-looking knife (Buñuel notes, "Such knives are found everywhere in Spain"). As Viridiana moves from the conventional Christianity of the convent to her own less institutionalized attempts with the beggars to the card game with Jorge she moves from death toward life.

Yet Jorge himself is something less than life even though he is able to enjoy working, eating, making love, and even though he does get some things accomplished on the estate. His limits are symbolized in the scene where he purchases and thus rescues a bedraggled, tired dog tied behind a wagon. As he turns his back and walks away, another similar wagon goes past with another similar dog tied in the same predicament.

The Last Supper *cum* orgy is Buñuel's vision of the

possibilities of Christianity beyond the limits of the bishops and the convents. A blind Christ who is even less than his fellows presides over a gala mockery. Buñuel's perception of the limits of Christianity are spelled out in the following exchange with an interviewer, Elena Poniatowska:

> Buñuel: Christ was crucified after He was found guilty. Wouldn't you call that a failure? Do you believe it is possible to be a Christian in the *absolute* sense of the word?
>
> Poniatowska: Yes, by giving up everything, by withdrawing from the world.
>
> Buñuel: No, no! I'm speaking of the *world,* of this earth on which we live. If Christ were to return, they'd crucify Him again. It is possible to be *relatively* Christian, but the *absolutely* pure, the *absolutely* innocent man—he's bound to fail. He's licked before he starts. I am sure that if Christ came back, the Church, the powerful Churchmen, would condemn Him again.[8]

For Buñuel, the most viable alternative is sadism, a philosophical sadism, not the sadism of pop analysis. He proposes an anarchistic explosion rooted in the complete lack of inhibition, the complete freedom of emotion and desire. Whatever blocks this development, by force or by ideology, must be destroyed. The choice is life or death, and Christianity, unknown and impossible in its pure form, has prostituted itself irrevocably to the service of death; the bishops and their mass are the vanguard of the Majorcans.

In summary, I feel that Buñuel says much that is of critical importance for those who still opt for Christianity, even though he doesn't see it as a live option. By way of his devastating, shaking "grotesque-ing" of institutionalized Christianity *and* of Christian ideals, he can perhaps help us to regain and refocus the key theological questions in a meaningful way. Particularly, he puts to us the unresolved question as to whether or not it is possible to live as a Christian without withdrawal, that kind of withdrawal on which non-acculturated Christianity so often seems to border.

Secondly, when he says: "Mystery interests me. Mystery is the essential element," and: "I am still, thank God, an atheist. I believe that one must search for God in man," it seems to me that there is surely no reason for a theology that is rooted in anthropology, anthropology under the shadow of the *mysterium,* to struggle against him.[9]

Finally, in criticism of Buñuel I must say that I see no indications that sadism—even of the philosophical variety—is a key to cosmic health. It would seem to have no more likelihood of realization than pure Christianity; also, it is much closer to irrationalism than to a balanced view of man which would give the reason its due.

Federico Fellini

> I decided to go with them. The ship was carrying a cargo of luxury goods and slaves. We anchored off ports unknown to me. . . . I heard for the first time the names of Kelisia . . . Rectis. . . . On an island covered by high sweet-scented grasses a young Greek introduced himself and told me that in the year . . .
>
> —Encolpius, speaking the closing
> lines of Fellini's *Satyricon*

A consistent characteristic of Fellini's films has been his fascination with grotesques: monstrously fat whores, strange fish, clowns of all kinds (thus his recent documentary on this subject), dwarfs, old crones, limbless torsos, strapping amazons, transvestites, cripples, hermaphrodites. All manner of humanity, the bizarre, the wonderfully fantastic—all these and more decorate his films, are woven in and out of them. However, in sheer number and variety of such types, *Satyricon* far outdoes any of Fellini's previous works. Their purpose, I believe, is clearly indicated.

Federico Fellini's biography in general and his artistic career specifically are fascinating; it is tempting to spend much more time with him and his work than is allowable here. This examination of his work is very limited, seeking to make but one point: Fellini uses the grotesque in "sportive" fashion, to fascinate, to draw us in and through his dreams to a new and fuller vision of life. In his work we encounter an emphasis on the experience of the *mysterium . . . fascinans.*

Fellini was born into the Italian bourgeoisie in Rimini in 1920. His first and unceasing love has been show business; this was indicated even before he ran away from home at the age of twelve to join a circus. Since then he has worked in a wide variety of jobs within the show business field. He worked as an artist for Italian illustrated magazines; wrote for the theater and acted; during the war he wrote for radio; he once made his living as a caricaturist in Roman restaurants. In the film world he moved from gag writer to adapter to script writer, working with Rossellini, Germi, and others. Finally, in 1950 he got his first chance to direct, making the film *Luci del Varieta.* Since then he has dealt with a variety of subjects and there has emerged a brilliant and remarkably consistent volume of films, including *I Vitelloni, La Strada, The Swindler, Nights of Cabiria, La Dolce Vita, 8 1/2,*

Juliet of the Spirits, Satyricon, The Clowns, and *Roma.*
It is *Satyricon,* a recent feature, that will serve as our
focus.

A synopsis of the film is difficult. Roughly and freely
the work is adapted from those remaining fragments of
Petronius Arbiter's classic on decadent Rome, supple-
mented by the director's extensive knowledge of the remains—literary and otherwise—of his ancestral culture
and by numerous significant studies of that past on which
Fellini has drawn. However, it is difficult to conceive of
this work as simply another of those studies; rather, it
must be understood as a study of Fellini, of us, of Western culture at this point, not back there, then. Further,
it is a strange, intensely interior study of us. It is, in Fellini's words, "a documentary of a dream."

The story, even more so than other works by Fellini,
rambles in a non-plot to no conclusions (offering conclusions Fellini has said he believes to be immoral). The
story happens around the wanderings and adventures of
three youths—Encolpius, Ascyltus, and Giton. Vignettes
are built around them and the characters they meet—
Eumolpus, the poet; Vernachio, the actor; Trimalchio,
the wealthy freedman, and his wife, Fortunata; Lichas,
the shipowner, and his wife, Tryphaena; the empress; the
sorceress, Oenothea; the minotaur; and many others, great
and small. Interwoven, complicating all, are not only the
junctures between these people but also the stories they
tell. There is Trimalchio's banquet; his mock funeral;
the collapse of the Insula Felicles; the Villa of Suicides;
the wild happenings on Lichas' ship; the assassination of
the emperor; the capture of the oracular hermaphrodite;
the weird "funeral" of Eumolpus—the list goes on.

What holds this non-story in place? Very little, unless

one approaches it as Fellini's documentary of a dream, a
dream that goes into the heart of our culture, now. And
the key to this dream may well be found in Fellini's grotesques and those grotesque happenings with which Fellini illuminates the screen, and would, perhaps, illuminate us.

It is important to understand that *Satyricon* is of a
piece with the other works of this director. For example,
let me relate it to Fellini's earlier *La Dolce Vita,* a film
that is a surpassingly powerful examination of the reality
and potency of modern nihilism. Yet the nihilism, however real its portrayal in *La Dolce Vita,* was not Fellini's
nihilism. Nor was it, as many critics suggested, the de-
cadence of Roman contemporary high society which was
depicted. Rather, like *Satyricon, La Dolce Vita* also is a
documentary of a dream. Repeatedly, it moves from the
world of realism toward the world of dreams; thus,

> the highly artificial composition of many of the shots, the
> complete antithesis of unvarnished actuality; the bold use
> of symbolic trappings like the deceptive echo-chamber
> from which Marcello makes his proposal to Maddalena;
> the occasional excursions into complete fantasy like the
> instantaneous and in this instance overtly subjective
> dawn over the fountain of Trevi. And yet, and yet . . .[10]

For Fellini, it is not primarily a matter of saying that
some people have accepted the bitter dictum, *nihil est,*
nothing has meaning. Nor is Fellini making the judgment that people should—or should not—arrive at that
conclusion. Rather, the most important level of meaning
in the film goes beyond this and tells us that life itself,
with ourselves within it, part of it, is terrifying, macabre,
grotesque. And how does it end?—with the dead fish's

dead eye? With the attempt to return to a long-dead purity? With a return to innocence, to the little girl across the inlet? Fellini does not say. It is not for him to say, he tells us. Rather, it is for us to live out the dream, each as best he can, with grace toward himself and toward others.

It is only in degree, not in kind, that *Satyricon* stands out among Fellini's films. It is *more* of a dream documentary, it is *more* replete with grotesques; in fact, the film as a whole is grotesque. Yet it must be held in continuum with his other work.

In an interview with Fellini, Alberto Moravia argues that *Satyricon* contains Fellini's vision of the present removed to the past. He tells Fellini that he has performed a "dream operation in reverse," in which he has played out his understanding of our present as though it were a monstrous antiquity, innocent in its admixture of the hideous and the beautiful. In spite of this innocence, Moravia argues that the vision of the present which Fellini dreams is that of a physical inferno "without purgatory and without paradise." [11] Moravia is right in suggesting that Fellini is concerned with the present, not the past as a thing unto itself, and he is right that an understanding of the film requires reference to the Freudian libido.

But Fellini with his very positive figures, his life symbols like Gelsomina (*La Strada*) and Cabiria (*Nights of Cabiria*) and Juliet (*Juliet of the Spirits*) and the little girl across the inlet (*La Dolce Vita*), is no pessimist, not even in *La Dolce Vita,* much less in *Satyricon*. And his director's eye is as gentle with his monsters as with the beautiful Giton. That is to say that Fellini is not in horror of the depths in self or cultures—even though they are beyond managing, for from out of these depths springs life itself. He who will go into the depths may live—or he may not. But there is nothing else to do, nowhere else to go; it is not given to stop and claim that life can be at rest in some *status quo* of our choosing; to stop is to die. Thus the significance of Encolpius' final speech is that he opts for life, with all its marvels and its rough edges, within and without. He says, "I decided to go with them."

Fellini tells us that the grotesques are part of us, that our world, like that of *Satyricon,* is grotesque. But for Fellini, the grotesque is more beautiful than ugly, more fascinating than fearful. Within it, out of it, is life itself, a life beyond reason. Only the individual, only the cultures which can meet and embrace the grotesque within can touch the source from which there can be movement toward wholeness of life.[12]

Postscript on Film

As I have written elsewhere, I believe that the cinema is the most powerful art form of our time and can offer us insights for regaining those key questions which Tillich tells us we've lost.[13] Thus there are a considerable number of other directors than Buñuel and Fellini whose work we could consider, with profit, if space allowed. I would like to close this section with several suggestions of other materials that support the argumentation I have been pursuing.

The films of Ingmar Bergman are of particular theological significance, not simply because this son of a Lutheran pastor seems haunted by the explicitly theological issues with which he frequently deals (often using rather traditional religious symbolism) but also because of the flirtation with the grotesque which recurs in his films. Film is that medium which perhaps better than any other allows the artist to express the sense of mystery that he has encountered in life. Not only Buñuel, who mentions his attraction to mystery, but all great directors have conveyed this sense of awe and wonder which begins at the limits of words. For Bergman, this sense is frequently played out in images of the grotesque.

A few examples from his classic, *The Seventh Seal,* should serve to illustrate. The knight, Antonius Block, and his squire, Jöns, are on their way home from a crusade; they have returned to a Sweden beset by the plague. The story is unfolded, on one level, by means of a chess game between the knight and Death, who is personified in as grotesque an image as appears in film, an eerie reminder of the reality of that death whose repression twists us into its worship. Further, death is considered explicitly in Jöns's dialogue with an artist in a little church later on when Jöns asks the artist why he is painting a grotesque Gothic dance of death. The artist (Bergman?) says, "I thought it would serve to remind people that they must die." [14]

At the close of the film there is that unforgettable image of the dance of Death, six figures led by the black reaper himself. "They dance away from the dawn and it is a solemn dance toward the dark lands, while the rain washes their faces and cleans the salt of the tears from their cheeks." [15] Solemn though this dance is, with it comes the cleansing rain; this scene with its crisp black-and-white silhouettes is in sharp contrast to the gray and morbid processional of flagellants portrayed earlier in the film in their macabre flight from the severe master. The scene with the flagellants, the monk, and his sermon is sharply removed from and opposed to the dance of death and Jof's description of it with which Bergman closes this masterpiece.

Through his grotesques, Bergman reminds us of the futility of our repression of death. Bergman's *The Seventh Seal,* like Brown's *Life Against Death,* confronts us again with the choice of a dualism or a dialectic of the life and death instincts.

Finally, I would like to suggest that there is need for theological concern with the common film genre of mystery and the grotesque, that is, the horror film.[16] The fascination that these films hold for young and old alike is acknowledged to be considerable, and various explanations have been offered for this. Perhaps this genre and its grotesques and their vast appeal would reward theological examination.

6

The Grotesque in Other Arts:
Picasso and Ionesco

My purpose is not to present an exhaustive analysis—or
even catalog—of the grotesque in contemporary culture.
Rather, I am simply pointing to the abundance of the
grotesque and suggesting that a theology which is anthropology, a theology which seeks to attest to the reality of
the Unconditional in the conditional, a theology which
seeks to break the chains of a rationalistic technological
society, would be a theology aware of and open to the
parallel movements in its culture. This must not be a
theology which asks, How can I use de Kooning or Giacometti or the like to illustrate my theology? but rather a
theology which asks, What is the truth about man which
this art attests?

Via the grotesque the arts not only speak to us of moral
outrage but also speak implicitly—and sometimes explicitly—of the mysterious experience of that which
shakes and fascinates, of the reality of the numinous in
our midst, and of the healing forces that the experience
of the numinous can awaken in us. The artist perhaps

can help open us to the health in the unconscious and lead us into the exploration of new possibilities, beyond reason and beyond technique. Can we be the pupils of the arts—which are all religious in their origins—as we seek the rebirth of a theology that can speak meaningfully to man in his brokenness, telling him that he is not alone and that he may yet become whole beyond reason?

Painting and Sculpture

> The dreams of reason produce monstrosities.   —Goya

> Only the cry of anguish can bring us to life.   —Camus

The grotesque in the arts of painting and sculpture can of course be traced back into the dimmest reaches of the history of the race; its prominence is attested by every variety of primitive art, particularly by those weird, fantastic cultic masks which are to be found from the Tlingit in Alaska to the Sepik in New Guinea, among the Ibo in Nigeria and the Tucuna in the Amazon.[1]

But the grotesque cannot be attributed to the "superstitions" of those we judge to be less civilized. As was noted above, the term itself comes from the Roman Empire at a time when that civilization could scarcely be called primitive. Further, as has been conclusively demonstrated in the critical studies of the grotesque by Kayser and Clayborough, the grotesque has increased in incidence and intensity in the art of Western culture since the scientific revolution and the triumph of rationalism until it has attained an unparalleled scope and ferocity in the twentieth century. Simply to chronicle the grotesque in the art of the past few centuries would be a staggering task; at this point we can only indicate its abundance and continue to suggest its significance.

Any list of the precursors of modern grotesque art should include Bosch's works such as *Garden of Earthly Delights* and *The Temptation of St. Anthony*; Arcimboldo with his double images; Raphael's frescoes; Hogarth's etchings; Brueghel; Blake; Goya; Füssli; Daumier; Callot; and many others. One might begin the survey of more recent grotesques with the early works of the Flemish artist James Ensor and his *Mask of Death* (1890) or his *Skeletons Disputing Before a Hanged Man* (1891). Ensor conveys grotesqueness not only explicitly through the masks his people are made to wear but also "by a new technique of breaking up and splicing lines which enabled him to express the malevolence of the world of objects and the ominously fantastic nature of space in a striking manner." [2]

Alfred Kubin (*Bad Luck Compounded, Giant Weasel*), who with Ensor initiates the explicitly grotesque in modern art, speaks of his work and its motivation thus:

> At times I was totally dominated by the urge to yield, even when conscious, to the nocturnal visions, and the impressions of the real world reached the core of my being as if deflected by some strange ground lenses.[3]

He stresses the feeling of a motivating impetus outside himself, impinging on him. Still Kubin's paintings were always bound to external reality, though piercing the surface of it.

By the early 1890's Ensor and Kubin respectively had presented visions of the grotesque and terrifying in the human world and in nature. In the years that followed, as the character of the twentieth century unfolded, these perspectives were expanded and amplified by a veritable army of artists.

One of the most significant developments in grotesque

art in these years was the explosion of dadaism on the European scene in the period extending from 1916 to 1919. An aggressively negativistic movement, the thrust of dada may be described accurately by borrowing from Rudolf Otto's discussion of the demonic phase of the numinous: "a suprarational identification of good and evil in an Indifferent . . . fundamentally independent of moral elevation or righteousness . . . indifferent toward good or evil . . . a ferocity, a fiery wrath about something unknown, or better still not about anything at all, but wrath on its own account." [4] The effect of this brief outburst was an abrupt dissociation from the accepted rules of art, illustrated, for example, by the antics of Marcel Duchamp, who once signed a rotating bottle drier and a bicycle wheel; entered a porcelain urinal entitled *Fontaine* and signed "R. Mutt" in a New York exhibit; and sent a snow shovel, a typewriter cover, and a hatrack to an exhibition featuring Matisse and Picasso.

Duchamp has been called by some the architect of dada, by others its demolition expert. In his words, dada was a useful and necessary purgative, a way to get rid of those states of mind which our culture had come to expect we must assume. Dada attempted by every means, conceivable and inconceivable, to create the *tabula rasa*, the unmarked mind Locke insisted was our birthright. By bizarre buffoonery (Paris dadaists once gave an exhibition that one could enter only by way of a urinal) and by a violent, almost dangerous rejection of the world forced on us by the assumption that all of life, and even art as well, must follow conventions and structures, the dadaists sought to free art of clichés and life of artiness.

Francis Picabia's famous *Dada Picture* illustrates clearly the dadaists' iconoclastic attack on academicism.

This piece consists of a toy monkey nailed to a canvas; around it are the words "Portrait de Rembrandt," "Portrait de Renoir," "Portrait de Cézanne," and so on. Picabia is saying that to ape the past, even its high accomplishments, is senseless; destruction must precede any new and genuine freedom.

This mad outburst was short-lived; negativism, shock value, and polemic could hardly be expected to be sustained as ends in themselves. But dada did make important contributions by refusing the chains of the old dogmas of art and culture, thus making possible later developments. Particularly, its uncompromising emphasis on givenness and actuality made it increasingly difficult for people to escape into what was *supposed* to be according to the deadly mores of Western culture.

The grotesques developed by George Grosz, one of the many artists to go through the experience of dadaism, are, I believe, of particular significance for us because there are inescapable parallels between the world of Weimar Germany that he describes in his drawings and in his biography, *A Big No and a Little Yes,* and our own time. The intertwining of capitalistic commercialism, depersonalized sex, and death recurs throughout such works of his as *Genre, For This He Cheated All Day, Early Awakening, Cross-Section, People at Cannes,* and many others. Grosz describes his horrendous *Germany, A Winter's Tale* thus:

"... the eternal German bourgeois. Fat and filled with anxiety, he sits in the center of the picture at a slightly unsteady table. In front of him are his cigars and morning newspaper. At the bottom are represented the three pillars of society: church, school and the army. The bourgeois is holding a knife and fork with great tension. The world is swaying about him. A sleeping dog at the right represents a filthy conscience that has fallen asleep. A prostitute, and a sailor, symbolizing the revolution, complete the picture." [5]

One cannot enter Grosz's world without feeling its discomforting contemporariness and the harsh reality that *homo consumens* may not forage forever with impugnity. Man is not alone, Grosz tells us—without resorting to Billy Graham's theodicies.

When one thinks of grotesque art in the twentieth century, surrealism, a movement broader than the graphic arts, comes to mind most readily.[6] One of the basic sources of surrealist ideas and artists was dadaism; perhaps one can begin to get into an understanding of surrealism by thinking of it as the emergence of the "yes" from the dadaist "NO-yes" symbol (in which a small "yes" was printed inside the "O" of a large "NO"). That is, while dadaism was a basically negative movement that sought to annihilate the old clichés and conventions, surrealism was an attempt to move beyond this, beyond destruction, in order to take up the task of finding new sources for rebirth, new wellsprings from which there might develop not only a new art but also a new society.

As is the case with most self-consciously intellectualistic movements that pass through many phases of development, it is difficult to establish a clear and concise definition of surrealism. As the term itself indicates, surrealism involves a quest for the real beyond the real. The structured and reasoned world that Western culture, via Plato's charioteer, has imposed on us is real in the sense that we constantly encounter it; it constantly impinges on us. Yet, according to the surrealists, this world is real only in a penultimate sense. The ultimate reality, the true reality, lies beyond it, but is accessible if we can break the bonds of this penultimate. Surrealism was an all-embracing, all-consuming quest for the means into the surreal, the ultimate. All its efforts reflect this quest and/or suggest the nature of the true reality beyond the penultimate reality of the conventional.

Man is the center of this quest: *"Au centre du monde est l'homme."* The most vital part of man is the interior, the subconscious. The way into this interior is paved by the sensual, and the way emerges into the sensual. The automatic, the fortuitous, the changing are that which must be sought, for only thus can one be free of the binding constraints of the past, the ever-new constraints of the present, and the lurking constraints of the future. Surrealism is ever in quest of the ever-moving limits of existence.

The juxtaposition of the absurd and the absolute and the non-rational and the unconscious in this movement seems to make it particularly significant for our considerations. However, there are certain factors which at the same time indicate the limits of its value and the causes of its decline. First, surrealism involved not only an openness to the non-rational but a glorification of the irrational, an impossible thrust outside the rational and the non-rational. Such irrationalism is as much an attempt to exceed the limits of being human as is rationalism.

A second and related criticism must be directed against surrealism's attempt to make absurdity the basis of their system; as Wolfgang Kayser notes in *The Grotesque in Art and Literature,* this attempt is absurd in itself.[7] Third, there is no small weight to O. F. Beer's caustic comment that the surrealists (he seems to have Dali in mind particularly) didn't get beyond the first fifty pages

of Freud's *Interpretation of Dreams*. Beer comments:
"A type of painting which limits itself to projecting half-
understood dream symbols onto the canvas, without spiritually digesting them, cannot fulfill its artistic function." [8]

Finally, when surrealism adopted Marxism, it fell victim to the process of politicization, the fallacies of which
Ellul has shown with such accuracy. In spite of lingering
purists and attempted revivals, surrealism seems to have
been, like dadaism, significant more because it helped
clear the way for new possibilities and new perceptions
than because of the possibilities or perceptions it brought
to birth by itself.

However, surrealism, including its grotesques, has con-
tributed to the twentieth-century attempts to heal man
of his repressions, to oppose the strictures of rationalism
and return to the Absolute. The grotesques of surrealism
as presented in the well-known paintings of Dali and
Magritte and de Chirico do indeed mix the familiar and
the fantastic in such fashion as to pull us out beyond
everyday "realism" and reasoned logic.[9] Via disruption
of accustomed context and unexpected new juxtapositions, they seek to thrust us into new insights, even beyond our seeking or desiring them.[10]

There are in surrealism these two related objectives:
a disruption of accepted reality so that sur-reality rather
than our concepts about reality may be experienced
anew, and the evocation of the mystery of the unconscious. According to the surrealists, these objectives
would bring us a renewed experience of "some nou-
menon," a renewed growth of a "cosmic consciousness."

Thus surrealists can speak of their work as an effort to
recover within the individual his awareness of his nou-

menal nucleus. They seek to explore the grotto of the unconscious in order to release the energies and insights that conventions and traditions of rationalism have forced to huddle there. The goal is nothing less than the resuscitation of man. It is in quest of these ends and in expression of the corresponding moods that the surrealist artists have given us their fantastic array of grotesque images.

However, it has not only been men devoted to the grotesque, such as Ensor or Kubin, nor the movements of dadaism and surrealism which indicate the significance of this mode of expression in modern art. Rather, from impressionism through the current fadist "Impossible Art," from Van Gogh through Willemijn Brattinga-kooy, the grotesque recurs in a fantastic variety in the art of our time. Particularly, those artists who feel the dehumanization of man under the onslaughts of technology have used the grotesque to cry out their protest and call for a rebirth of man. Such artists make up a veritable roll call of the contemporary masters, including Picasso, Kokoschka, Muncy, Rouault, Kandinsky, Dubuffet, Bacon, Mueller, and Golub in painting as well as Giacometti, César, Baskin, Armitage, Wotruba, Roszak, Westermann, Paolozzi, and Richier in sculpting. All these and more thrust before us their strange, elongated, contorted, squashed figures protesting that man under technique is no longer man.

Let us examine one specific painter and one specific painting in order to draw out more precisely the role in which the grotesque may function in contemporary art. Let us examine Picasso's famous *Guernica*.

The artist, the painting, and the situation that gave rise to it are well known. Guernica was a small Basque town in northern Spain, in the province of Bilbao. During the Spanish civil war, fought by Spanish fascists supported by the fascist governments of Germany and Italy against the ruling loyalist government with its leftist leanings and leftist allies, this town had the tragic misfortune of becoming a point of dispute. On the afternoon of April 28, 1937, the town came under heavy air attack by combined German and Italian forces. Guernica became the first victim of saturation bombing, i.e., bombing which has as its aim to leave nothing alive or usable.

Two days later, Picasso began work on his painting *Guernica*. Involving many sketches that indicate and illuminate his considerations at this time, Picasso completed this work about June 15. The painting, monumental in style and size and content, has been considered a masterpiece since it was first shown at the Spanish government pavilion at the Paris World's Fair in 1937.

Guernica is painted on canvas, and is done entirely in black and white and gray. Though *Guernica* is probably the best-known twentieth-century painting, Alfred Barr's concise and accurate description is worth repeating at this point:

> One sees: at the right two women, one with arms raised before a burning house, the other rushing in toward the center of the picture; at the left a mother with a dead child, and on the ground the fragments of a warrior, one hand clutching a broken sword. At the center of the canvas is a dying horse pierced by a spear hurled from above; at the left a bull stands triumphantly surveying the scene. Above, to the right of the center a figure leans from a window holding a lamp which throws an ineluctable light upon the carnage. And over all shines the radiant eye of day, with the electric bulb of night for a pupil.[11]

This is the work that Tillich acclaimed as the greatest religious painting of the twentieth century.

The immediate impression one receives on viewing *Guernica* is that it is a grotesque and terrifying conglomeration of pieces. Pieces of the living and the dead, the human and the animal, the organic and the inorganic, appear in rampant confusion across the face of the canvas. Nothing fits, there is no order, all is chaos and destruction, there is no meaning. The immediate interpretation one gives to the painting is that this is a rather blunt and simple, but exceptionally powerful, statement against the brutality and inhumanity of war. It appears to be a direct, passionate cry against the senselessness of the bombing of the Spanish town.

The immediate impression and the immediate interpretation are right: *Guernica* is indeed exactly these things. But it is also much more. In view of the preceding argumentation concerning reason and the grotesque and in view of related Picasso works from the same period, this "much more" emerges. Let us now probe the painting in greater detail through a consideration of four of its major elements: the woman with the lamp, the wounded horse, the crushed warrior, and the bull.[12]

The wounded horse just at the left of center is one of the focal points of the picture which immediately catches the eye. This is not a realistic element relating to the bombing of Guernica, but is a recurrent motif in several of Picasso's works from the period 1933–1937, which culminates in this masterpiece. In an ink drawing, *Bullfight*, from 1934, there is a very similar horse that has been grotesquely wounded by a bull. A similar horse recurs throughout several bullfight compositions from this time and appears also in the etching *Minotauromachy*, from 1935. Throughout these works there recurs the figure of a woman onlooker much like the woman with the lamp in *Guernica*. Thus Picasso has been struggling with this trio—horse and woman and bull—for some time. The mood pervading these works is a mixture of myth and fantasy and nightmare; one senses several possible layers of meaning.

It has been suggested that the horse serves as a symbol for the feminine principle and feminine attributes. More specifically, as is frequent in art and literature, this feminine symbol here serves as locus for the "feminine" attribute of suffering.[13]

The woman with the lamp is also a recurrent figure in the Picasso works from this period, including *Minotauromachy* and *Bullfight*. Further, she appears as a basic figure throughout the sketches done for *Guernica*, though the figure itself and the light appear in varied styles and forms. She appears always as an onlooker, a spectator, even as she is in the figure cast out over the pieces and horror of *Guernica*. She is not one of those upon whom suffering has been inflicted, but she is over and above the chaos and pain. In her face we see the response of reason whose suffering is only that of one whose well-knit schemes have broken asunder. Is she Athena, goddess of wisdom, whose lamp, the light of reason, cannot pierce the grays and blacks beneath her? The lamp lit at noonday does not suffice.

What is one to make of the fallen warrior? Are there any clues to his meanings? Again, the grotesque and fragmented figure becomes quite intelligible in the context of Picasso's life and his earlier work. Picasso received his early art education in the manner typical of his time. The art studios in which he began his training were generally equipped with plaster models of the great art of classical antiquity. The thinking behind such education as this appears to have paralleled the thinking so typical of Western culture generally: Out of an understanding of first principles, long established and inviolable, one will learn all he needs to know.

However, we know that Picasso, like so many other artists of the twentieth century, reacted rather violently against this approach. He writes:

> Academic training in beauty is a sham. We have been deceived, but so well deceived that we can scarcely get back even a shadow of the truth. The beauties of the Parthenon, Venuses, Nymphs, Narcissuses, are so many lies. Art is not the application of a canon of beauty but what the instinct and the brain can conceive beyond any canon.[14]

Picasso also reacted against this approach with his works, as one can see in such examples as *Studio* (1925); *Plaster Arm* (1893–1894); and *The Torso* (1933) in which, in varying degrees, he parodies his plaster-cast, first-principles education.

Thus the fallen warrior of *Guernica,* whose right arm definitely looks as though it came from an ancient statue, is not so much a human fragment as a broken bit of statue from classical antiquity. It symbolizes the mainstream of Western tradition, that "old bitch gone in the teeth," made up with reasons and necessary truths. This analysis is further strengthened both by the fact that the figure holds a sword (anachronistic in 1937) and by the fact that one of the sketches for *Guernica* shows this prostrated warrior wearing a helmet of the type from classical antiquity.

It was not simply the Spanish Loyalist who fell at

Guernica; rather, in the happening of Guernica we have illustrated that juncture at which Western culture stands. The toppling of the hopes of the whole tradition of necessary truths and inviolable reasons is startlingly manifest. The inadequacy, the meaninglessness of the basic presuppositions of our cultural mainstream, was laid bare there in the Basque in 1937—and in hundreds of unnamed towns annihilated since that time.

The final figure to concern us is the bull. As I have indicated, this figure also appears in several of Picasso's works of this period. In addition to those mentioned above, there is his cover for the magazine *Le Minotaure* in 1933, his *Minotaur and the Dying Horse* (1936), and his *Bull's Head,* a bull figure done with human features in May of 1937. These works as well as sketches done for *Guernica* show that the Minotaur myth was prominent in Picasso's thinking at this time.

The Minotaur is the familiar half-human, half-bull monster from Greek mythology. He lived in a dark and intricate cave-like place called the Labyrinth, on Crete. Annually, Athenians had to send him a group of maidens and young men, who were placed in the Labyrinth and soon devoured by the monster. One year the Athenian prince, Theseus, was among them. There is the ancient story of Theseus slaying the Minotaur and, with the help of the Cretan princess, Ariadne, releasing the captives and heading home. However, Theseus deserted Ariadne on the isle of Naxos, where, legend has it, the princess became the bride of Dionysus, the Greek god of the creative passions, both good and evil.

As this single account indicates, the bull figure is a very old and very complex symbol with many facets, many layers of meaning. The symbol is found as far back as ancient Sumer, where the bull is a fertility symbol. It recurs throughout the ancient cultures in varied guises with varied roles. For example, in Phoenicia the bull-god, Moloch, received the sacrifice of newborn children; the mother with the dead child before the bull in *Guernica* reminds us of this also.

During this period around 1937, Picasso worked with these bull themes and others, seemingly giving his fantasy free play in sketches and paintings and etchings of a half-dream, half-nightmare, mythological character. His sketches for *Guernica* consistently show that he had settled on a bull figure from the beginning but that he considered presenting the bull in many ways—dull and stupid, hideous and monstrous, youthful and noble—before finally settling on the figure we see in *Guernica,* imposing, powerful, triumphant, animal but almost human.

There seems to be little room for doubt. In this bull figure, Picasso is drawing on the complex ancient mythological symbol, multifaceted, with many layers of meaning, half suggested, subconscious. The force of this figure is even more striking when we recall the rarity of mythological figures in modern art.

Why are mythological figures seldom encountered in the art of the past century? Are they not scarce because a rationalistic technological society has no need of myths, no room for myths; they are not factual, scientific, historical. They didn't happen. They are messy and nonrational, impossible to synthesize and summarize neatly— as the complexity of the bull symbol clearly shows. They are not true as reason counts truth. Idealized naturalistic paintings or even abstracts of lines and colors that firmly remain lines and colors are much preferred by the Muzak culture.[15]

But Picasso resurrects the ancient bull myths and allows the grotesque bull to dominate the scene at Guernica. This bull reminds us of the hidden forces within the labyrinths of the subconscious, individual and corporate, which will wreak their blind and destructive rage whenever we pretend that Plato's charioteer can and should rule. Beyond the realism of ideologies and reasons there is the super-real of myth and passion and the subconscious which cannot be enclosed within the caves forever. This bull, this hero-villain, this savior-destroyer, these creative-destructive forces and passions beyond reason remain glaring in cold triumph amid the broken plaster statues under the woman's ineffectual lamp.

Who is victim at Guernica? Who is victor? The question, finally, cannot be put that way. Picasso's masterpiece stands above all else as a grotesque reminder of the realities beyond reason, reason which has long since proved inadequate for the ascendancy to which she pretends. In spite of all our efforts, the repressed will return.

In conclusion of this glimpse at the graphic arts, the quest of so many contemporary painters and sculptors for a rebirth of man is described by Paul Tillich:

> They resist the temptation of tired relapses or premature solutions. They fight desperately over the image of man, and by producing shock and fascination in the observer, they communicate their own concern for threatened and struggling humanity. They show the smallness of man and his deep involvement in the vast masses of inorganic matter out of which he tries to emerge with toil and pain; they demonstrate the controlling power of technical forms over man by dissecting him into parts and re-constructing him, as man does with nature. They reveal the hidden presence of animal trends in the unconscious and the primitive mass-man from which man comes and to which

civilized mass-man may return. They dare to emphasize certain elements and parts of the natural figure and to leave out others in the desire to express something which nature hides. And if they depict the human face, they show that it is not simply given to us but that its human form itself is a matter of continuous struggle. There are demonic forces in every man which try to take possession of him, and the new image of man shows faces in which the state of being possessed is shockingly manifest. In others the fear of such possession or the anxiety at the thought of living is predominant, and again in others there are feelings of emptiness, meaninglessness and despair. But there are also courage, longing and hope, a reaching out into the unknown.[16]

Theology is bound to anthropology. It is only the God encountered in the twisted images of man as we know him in our time who can meet man in hope, in the unknown, but he who will not recognize the agony, who will not meet God in the agony of man, cannot do other than seek to disguise, briefly, the inhumanity of our technological society or, worse, offer the cheap hope of orthodoxy's god who will destroy the world in order to save it. These artists who thrust before us these fearful and fascinating images would, like Flannery O'Connor, lead us through the jaws of St. Cyril's dragon into new possibilities beyond reason. This, perhaps, is the route on which we may be met anew by the God of Abraham and Isaac and Jacob.

Music and Theater

The arts of the theater and music also attest to the powerful presence of the grotesque in our time. In music one can go back, for example, to Hector Berlioz and not only to some of his compositions but also to his collected literary works entitled *Les Grotesques de la Musique.* One can also think of Ravel's *Grotesque,* Alban Berg's *Wozzeck,* Carl Orff's *Carmina Burana,* and other works in this vein.

But perhaps the most significant composer for consideration would be John Cage. It is justifiable to compare Cage's work in music to the work of the dadaists and surrealists in art; his work is a revocation of the past with its music of ideas. But Cage may also be compared to those attempts in the graphic arts which seek to recapture meaning in the present. He achieves these accomplishments in sound by a grotesque obliteration of normal connections and expectations. Particularly significant is his use of silence. Again one is reminded of the words of Rudolf Otto: "Silence is what corresponds [to the use of darkness in art-architecture] in the language of music. . . . With prophet and psalmist and poet we feel the necessity of silence from another and quite independent motive. It is a spontaneous reaction to the feeling of actual *numen praesens.*" [17] Whereas the technological society literally cancels out silence, Cage recaptures it and recaptures the music of the ordinary by his bizarre clippings of sounds and silence.[18]

Also, the adjective "grotesque" may be used in the description of much of the recent hard rock and acid rock. Of particular significance in this regard is the work of such people as Frank Zappa, Jethro Tull, the Stones, and the Bonzo Dog Band.

When one turns to the theater, one encounters a great many examples of the grotesque; the very masks that are its symbols attest this. In pre-modern times, there was, for example, the *commedia dell'arte*. Then skipping up into our own century we find several movements that have used the grotesque, beginning with the Italian school, the *teatro del grottesco*, with its master, Luigi Pirandello; the theater of cruelty with Antonin Artaud as its spokesman; and particularly the theater of the absurd with Beckett, Ionesco, Pinter, Genêt, Grass, and others. According to Friedrich Dürrenmatt, the grotesque tragicomedy is the only legitimate genre for our times.[19]

The term "theater of the absurd" has come to designate the works by dramatists who have sought by both content and form to break with the traditional concepts of drama. Ionesco and the others grouped in this "school" feel that traditional concepts of drama have come to reduce a total intuition of being to conceptual terms, neatly packaged in characters whose situations were "plausibly" explained and, generally, "plausibly" resolved in the final act.

The theater of the absurd has involved a kind of Punch and Judy assault on the conventional wisdom which can work only insofar as we maintain a pretend world in which reason is god and technology his lead-footed angel who will trample out his paths—even through living flesh. The theater of the absurd would lead us to the real outside the realm of rational experience and beyond the grasp of intellectual solution. It would teach us to feel anew the meaninglessness of our culture and its trends, and it would tacitly remind us that beyond our managing there is meaning. Thus this theater, as caustic and grinding as it may be, would restore to the drama its original religious functions. As a representative of the theater of the absurd and its grotesques, let us consider Eugène Ionesco's play *The Bald Soprano*, a simple, well-known and effective example of this movement.

A bit of background on the man and the play is particularly important in this case. Ionesco was born in 1912 in Slotina, Romania, of a French mother and a Romanian father. Most of his youth was spent in France, and French is his first language.

As a child in Paris, Ionesco was particularly affected by the Punch and Judy shows which his mother took him to see at the Luxembourg Gardens. Recalling these experiences, he says, "It was the spectacle of the world itself, which unusual, improbable, but truer than truth, presented itself to me in an infinitely simplified and caricatured form, as if to underline its grotesque and brutal truth." [20]

His early impressions of life as fraught with anxiety, brutality, and chaos seem to have remained with him. However, as he grew older, his relationship with the theater changed. He came to have a strong dislike for it because of the disparity between the impoverished and broken world of the real, live actors whom he knew as an adult and the world of the imagination which they sought to present on the stage. For Ionesco, theater came to be "an embarrassing spectacle" because of this disparity.

Ionesco married; he went to work for a publishing house. He enjoyed cinema, music, and art, but he found himself quite alienated from the theater. In 1948 at the age of thirty-six, there was no indication that he would become a playwright.

His change in vocation happened in a most curious way. He decided to learn English, and set about to do so through the use of a book entitled *L'Anglais sans peine*.

His explanation of this experience thrusts us into the heart of his thought and also provides something of a synopsis for *The Bald Soprano*. Ionesco tells us that his English primer taught him some astonishing truths: "There are seven days in a week." "The floor is down, the ceiling up." Characters were introduced into the primer, a Mr. and Mrs. Smith and a Mr. and Mrs. Martin. They also deal in the profound, telling themselves that they are married, that they live in such and such a house, that they have so many children.

Concerning this, Ionesco writes: "I should like to point out the irrefutable, perfectly axiomatic character of [the] assertations, as well as the entirely Cartesian manner of the author of my English primer, for what was truly remarkable about it was its eminently methodical procedure in its quest for truth. . . . Starting from basic axioms, they build more complex truths: 'The country is quieter than the big city.' " [21]

This English primer "in the Cartesian manner" contained the basis of dialogue for a drama and also seems to have helped clarify for Ionesco what he had long felt to be the malaise behind the brutality and chaos of our time. Here were two couples, the Martins and the Smiths, in the most reasonable, logical, and sober way systematically explaining away any possiblility of meaning or communication. The truisms and clichés were totally empty, but also they were frightening approximations to the day-by-day contacts of twentieth-century man.

Building on the foundations suggested by the primer, Ionesco went on to draw out a series of poetic images replete with pointless anecdotes and the most unfeeling automatism. One of the best-known examples is the lengthy dialogue between Mr. and Mrs. Martin in which,

by systematic and logical deduction, they are able to recognize that they are indeed husband and wife since they
live on the same street in the same apartment building
on the same floor in the same room where they sleep in
the same bed and share the same little daughter, Alice,
remarkable for the fact that she has one red eye and one
white eye. Another classic incident from the play is the
fire chief's pointless, endless story in which everyone is
named Bobby Watson, nothing happens, and there is no
significance. The play, in a sense, does not end. Having
reached a kind of non-conclusion, it simply begins over
again; it is circular. It could go on forever.

Why this assault on meaning and language? Why this
grotesquing of clichés and truisms into hyper-clichés and
hyper-truisms? Why the pointless anecdotes *ad infinitum?*
Contrary to much of the criticism of his work, Ionesco
does this not because he is abysmally pessimistic and
feels that all attempts at communication and meaning are
invalid from the start. As he has noted, if this were the
case, there would be no point in making any effort to
write. Rather, Ionesco seeks to break down the language
of logic and syllogisms and rules and conventions. He at-
tacks language of the mind which is not also language of
the heart.

The statement that he seeks to make in *The Bald Soprano* is not that we use clichés and have difficulty com-
municating. He seeks to go beyond this and communicate his own experience of what it *feels* like to be the object of a constant bombardment of "pre-packed, neatly
formulated conceptual pills." His efforts are directed toward the destruction of the rationalistic fallacy, droned
into each of us in the Cartesian manner, that language
alone apart from feeling and experience can establish any
communication of ultimate value and meaning.

However, in his grotesque use of language, it is not Ionesco's sole purpose simply to have us experience the inadequacy of the rationalistic approach. For him, language is not an end in itself but, growing out of experience, it is a means toward experience. Above all else, he is seeking to help us recover what he calls "the astonishment of being," a mystical, poetic intuition that there *is* a reality beyond the reality of the cog caught up in the technological world and its mechanized processes of production and consumption. His work is a call to this "astonishment of being" even in the face of the lack of any integrative principle which will underwrite our endeavors for us. As Martin Esslin notes, he is Zarathustra's old man who would make up songs and laugh and weep and growl.[22] If Ionesco does not do this in praise of the old, gone God, he does so out of his own felt awareness of the astonishment of being which impinges on us in spite of our reasons.

The grotesque is, in fact, all-pervasive in the arts of our era, so pervasive that it is beyond chronicling here; it can only be sampled. But such sampling and attempting to understand is not only possible but necessary if we are to understand our age and if we are to construct a theology that can speak to it. Our theology, if it is to be of any value, must be rooted deeply within the experience of man in our times, for it is here that the Unconditional, the *totaliter aliter,* the holy, the numinous, *is* encountered. Some artists will not let us forget this.

7

Hope Beyond Reason

A God comprehended is no God.   —Tersteegen

To find God, one must tear oneself from the seductions
of reason.   —Lev Shestov

By the continual living activity of its non-rational elements a religion is guarded from passing into rationalism.
                                    —Rudolf Otto

In the foregoing material it is argued that our contemporary history is the history of that rationalization of all
phases of existence which has issued in the sterility of our
technological society. Rationalism, it has been argued,
dominates not only secular life but religious life as well;
it has generally dominated not only orthodoxy but also
atheism and our attempts to strike out for new theological ground.

The exaltation of reason has involved the isolation of
the intellect in ancient Greece, the glorification of the
"scientific" methodology in the eighteenth century, and
the consequent industrialization-technologization of the

past two centuries. More significant than such developments without are their roots within. Psychoanalytically, the roots are deep within, in the cleft between the life instinct and the death instinct; the impossible flight from death becomes instead its adoration. Theologically, the roots are in our own constant re-enactment of the story of Adam and Eve, our choices of the tree of knowledge over the tree of life, with the resultant pride of management of all phases of existence. We are the grocers whom Zorba scorns, the grocers who, with cool reason, weigh the goodness, the badness, and necessities of Lidice and My Lai, Auschwitz and Hiroshima as well as a thousand other unnamed places that may await us in our future. Ultimately, life itself is subsumed under this weighing and measuring—and life vanishes in our quests for control.

Over against this dominance of death, beyond our ability to manipulate and manage, there stands even today—especially today—the non-rational experience of the *mysterium tremendum et fascinans,* the more-than-rational experience of that which shakes and fascinates beyond our ability to pinpoint and analyze and define and control the source. The reality of this experience is attested in the extremities of our rationalism by the grotesque in the arts and literature of our age, an age in which this genre flourishes. A theology that is rooted in anthropology cannot avoid attempting to come to grips with the grotesque.

Thus far we have noted the extensive abundance of the grotesque in our arts and literature and have explored and made suggestions concerning the significance of the grotesque in selected works of Flannery O'Connor, Buñuel and Fellini, Picasso and Ionesco. In this concluding chapter, let us push the questions a bit farther and consider these issues: Can one distinguish between the "good" and the "bad" grotesque? What, in summary, is the significance of the grotesque for our theology specifically and for our culture generally?

Good and Bad Grotesque?

A recurrent question in the history of theology, a question that can take a variety of forms, may be put in this oversimplified fashion, "How do you tell the good guys from the bad guys?" How do you tell the true prophet from the false prophet, the true spirit from the lying spirit, good faith from bad faith, the committed and concerned from the uncommitted and unconcerned? More specifically in relation to the subject matter discussed above, when is the grotesque a legitimate theological concern, or Christian, or constructive, or simply meaningful, and when is it not?

The answers to such questions, both within the Biblical materials and in the history of theology, have taken many different shapes. For Micaiah ben Imlah, even the false prophets are Yahweh's agents, tricking the Omrides into their downfall. Jeremiah, a few centuries later, offers suggestions but finally seems to flounder on the question; in any case, he seems to have lost his argument with Hananiah. The Deuteronomist admonishes that one wait and see what happens before one decides between the good and the bad. Luther simply thunders at Zwingli that he is not of the same spirit. The suggestions are almost as numerous as theologians.

Though the question is important, perhaps an answer is neither possible nor necessary. Perhaps the Deuteronomist, who suggests that we allow the events to proceed and unfold the true from the false, may have the most viable suggestion after all, in spite of being open to the charge that he offers us no solution in the immediacy of a crisis. However, if we go beyond this suggestion and try to formulate guidelines, they seem invariably to become rationalistic defenses that secure our own position and, in the process, again determine where the holy can be encountered, what it will say, and so on. If we are caught between the either-or of rationalistic defenses and the Deuteronomist's after-the-fact approach, the latter would certainly seem preferable. If one is not to lapse into such defense, one can offer only a few modest suggestions, but no formulas.

First of all, the fact that a specific instance of the grotesque is not Christian in origin or intent does not make it theologically invalid or negative or meaningless. In fact, as with Buñuel, the grotesque may be explicitly anti-Christian and, nonetheless, be of considerable theological significance.

Perhaps the negative or theologically "invalid" grotesque would be the grotesque bearing any or all of the following admittedly subjective characteristics:

1. Subservience to rationalism; i.e., the grotesque as a tool for an ideology dominated by propositional truths.

2. The grotesque without mystery, the grotesque used by people for purposes of manipulating others to their ends.

3. The grotesque that blocks the emergence of selfhood, individual identity and/or responsibility.

4. The grotesque that acquiesces to a dualism of the life instinct against the death instinct.

Current examples of such "negative" grotesques are to be found among such phenomena as cycle gangs, Satan cults, and the current rash of occultism.

On the other hand, characteristics of the positive or theologically "valid" grotesque would be basically the opposite of the above. Included would be:

1. An affirmation of an instinctual dialectic rather than an instinctual dualism.

2. An appeal to man in his totalness, including especially his non-rational factors.

3. The shattering of the securities that man seeks to build and guarantee on his own terms.

4. The evocation of mystery.

5. An address and/or appeal to the individual in his solitariness, *his* responsibility.

Examples are evident from the previous discussion.

These suggestions may be of value insofar as they are *not* formulas. Rather than asking after a timeless and universal delineation of the negative and/or positive aspects of the grotesque, we would do better to ask, "Why do I, as this particular individual, respond in such and such a fashion to this particular grotesque?" [1]

Theology and Art and the Grotesque

Since the material in Chapter 4 through Chapter 6 was the grotesque in the arts, perhaps it is worthwhile to underline again the value of such arts for theology. As has been noted by Dilthey, Tillich, and others, the true nature of theology closely approximates the nature of art. Theology, if it seeks to attest to the hidden, felt-rather-than-understood, heart of the human experience, more closely approximates art than philosophy. The arts themselves are religious in their origins and, if we can overcome our fragmentation-specialization with its separation of religion and life, perhaps we will again recognize the religiousness of art. Indeed, it may be only by returning to the arts that theology, encountering anew the attempts to express the *Grundlage,* the ultimate source, of human experience, may speak effectively of the healing of our fragmentation. Finally, theology may again become poetry—as it was for Hosea and Jeremiah and Koheleth.

Only as it more thoroughly distinguishes itself from rationalistic philosophy and more closely approximates art can theology begin to attest to the ramifications of the felt experience that the meaning of this world lies with what other ages have called "God." Perhaps if theology becomes again an art form, the theologian will be in a better position to speak of the experience of the *totaliter aliter* without pretending to know more about Him than He knows about Himself.

From this viewpoint, let us move into a summarization of the significance of the grotesque in art. For purposes of convenience and clarity, this discussion is divided, artificially, into the categories of man, God, and hope. We begin with man.

Man

All flesh is grass . . . —Isaiah 40:6

The overwhelming witness of the grotesque art in regard to man is that he is twisted, broken, fragmented. He seeks to cope with this brokenness particularly by way of his chrome-plated accouterments of progress which he would use to assure himself that he is headed in a valid direction—without ever asking what that direction might be. Related to this is his attempt to conceal this brokenness by hiding in groups. These two themes recur in grotesque art and literature; man is in flight from himself via things and/or groups. For example, the devaluation of the property answer is the theme of George Grosz's *Germany, A Winter's Tale,* while the infeasibility of the varied group answers plays throughout Fellini's *La Dolce Vita*; in both cases, a dominant aspect of these depictions of man is his fragmentation.

This depiction of the horrors of fragmentation is, of course, the counter side of the quest for wholeness. Further, the arts, particularly the grotesque in the arts, shout at us that wholeness is possible only if we recover what property and group seek to conceal. What they conceal is, above all, the reality of death and the limits of reason, that vice by which man would become as God, knowing good and evil.

In the words of Joseph Campbell, "Above all we need to be taught more affection for the infirmities of life." [2] Among the foremost of these "infirmities" are the facts that man is not, except perhaps in that most artificial Brave New World, his own source nor the final determinant of his own destiny. Theologically speaking, that is to say that man is not God. And, theologically speaking, the fierceness with which the arts portray man in his brokenness suggests than man's refusal of his conditionedness is generally understood as *threat* only because of the *feeling*—not the knowledge—that man is, ultimately, surrounded by the Unconditional. Without the experience of the Unconditional, the numinous, the *mysterium,* the acid wrath of the grotesque depiction of man in his brokenness is as meaningless as if one were to chastise an orange for not being an elephant. However, the arts remind us that we *do* know this brokenness and we *do* feel that this wrath, this fierceness, is fully appropriate.

Also among our basic "infirmities" is the simple actuality that man dies. Yet as Freud and others have shown, our inability to accept this infirmity, if it may be called that, results in our shattering obeisance to death which can end only in a final conflagration or in 1984. Unless we can recover the infantile *dialectic* of life and death, we cannot live.

Old Testament man who lived without absolutizing reason also lived without pretending he would not die. Likewise, Paul also refuses to take flight into hopes of immortality. Man dies; only against this background is the talk of resurrection meaningful in any sense. Further, for Paul the consequence of resurrection is not the restoration of my egocentric possibilities, the bridging of some sort of gap in my immortality, but the restoration of all things in the oneness of the Unconditional (I Cor. 15:28).

Perhaps deep within the mysteriousness of life there is the secret that death, the old adversary, is finally a friend. The sting of death leads from and to our alienation from life, life which never flowers because of our constant quest for escape from our great infirmities. But the secret of the Eastern nirvana concept and of the Biblical sabbath is the secret that he who can affirm life now, without flight from the past or attempts to control the future, can also die. Death is not the point at which, as Schopenhauer suggested, one ceases to be that which he had done better never to become, but rather the final rest of that which is full; as Nietzsche tells us, "All that is ripe wants to die." [3]

If we can learn more affection for our infirmities, for our "not-godness" and our death, we can perhaps recover the insight that Christianity is not a religion of immortality. Every belief in immortality is founded either in a rejection of these infirmities—and thus of the Unconditional—or in attempts to coerce the Unconditional to accept our will. The quest for immortality and the quest for the knowledge of good and evil coincide; they are, from the psychoanalytical and the theological perceptions respectively, the *Grundlage* of the technological society—and of its malaise. The truth of these perceptions and their counterpointing concerns for the wholeness of man are among the realities underlined by the grotesque in the modern arts. The power of these arts lies in their ability to address man as a totality beyond his brokenness.

The drive toward sameness in our culture, so obvious all about us, is challenged by this encounter with the grotesque. The artist of the grotesque, by severely readjusting and rearranging the people and the world that we constantly assume, thrusts before us perceptions other than those sanctified by consensual validation. Because these distortions relate to some uncomfortably real awareness inside of us, because we are able to feel that what they say must be dealt with—rejected or considered, but not ignored—they are able to challenge the uniformity of man in the technological society. They suggest that grotesqueness is something known within each of us, that there is something within each of us which answers to these grotesques, and they also remind us that the sameness of our society is not wholeness. At the same time, they hold out the hope that wholeness is a possibility.

In summary, the view of man offered via the grotesque is that man is broken and fragmented, mechanized, standardized. Further, this malaise issues out of man's flight from his death and from his not-godness which he would conceal via property and groups in a hopeless quest for immortality. In spite of the fervency and constancy of these quests, they do not succeed; rather, they spiral downward either to the literal oblivion of nuclear war or the bland oblivion of totalitarian megacountries.

God

Out of the depths I cry to thee, O Lord.   —Psalm 130:1

The desire to avoid the term "God" can be appreciated in view of its misuse in rationalistic theism, but we have not yet arrived at an acceptable substitute. Perhaps the cumbersome "whence of my being agitated," which Herbert Braun has suggested, is most helpful, particularly because it seems quite resistant to rationalistic abuse.[4] For Braun, the believing self-understanding is awakened in those events which thrust us before this whence, in the events of our being agitated. Thus there is not a theoretical knowledge of the whence but only the "event which occurs again and again. The truth of what we have traditionally called the God-man relation is bound to its being proclaimed anew, heard, heeded, actualized."[5]

"Man as man, man in relation with his fellow man, implies God," says Braun.[6] For the theologian who feels that this is a helpful mode or direction of talking, there can be no escape from the risk of attempting to interpret the meaning of man's culture, here, now. This is what it means to speak of a theology bound to anthropology. In such speaking one risks both a certain kind of ideological imperialism *and* theological inaccuracy, heresy, if you will—the theologian's occupational hazard.

The risk of speaking of the Unconditional in the conditional, the holy among men, is, finally, a vocation always on the edge of change, the very change from which ideological theism seeks to defend both itself and its Unmoved Mover. Bultmann's reminder of the need for openness is worth careful consideration. He states:

> It then remains to keep oneself open at any time for the *encounter with God in the world, in time.* It is not the acknowledgment of an image of God be it ever so correct, that is real faith in God; rather, it is the readiness for the eternal to encounter us at any time in the present—at any time in the varying situations of our life. Readiness consists in openness in allowing something really to encounter us that does not leave the I alone, the I that is encapsulated in its purposes and plans, but the encounter with which is designed to transform us, to make us ever new selves. The situation can be heartening just as well as disheartening, can be challenging as well as requiring endurance. What is demanded is selflessness, not as a pattern of moral behavior, but as the readiness not to cling to our selves, but to receive our authentic selves ever anew. This readiness can be interrogative, but it can also be completely naive. For surprisingly God can encounter us where we do not expect it.[7]

In view of the past close relationship of theology and the arts, we should not be surprised that the encounter might be renewed there, even in grotesques such as those of O'Connor and Fellini and Picasso and Buñuel.[8]

The powerful presentation of the agitation and of the very real agony of man in our time is undoubtedly one of the recurrent disturbing accomplishments of the grotesque in contemporary art and literature. The artist is not only saying that this is how modern man experiences himself and his life but also is raising the question of why? From Whence?

As the theologian takes up the question of the whence of his agitation, he moves into the realm of God-talk, God-talk like that of Augustine, who speaks of the God who pursues us in the restlessness of our hearts, and like that of Herbert Braun, who speaks of God as the ground of our being agitated. That is, the theologian may risk the interpretation that God himself is the source of man's anxieties which rise out of his flight from death and his claim to possess the knowledge of good and evil.[9]

In a sense, God is encountered as the enemy, as the one who will not let man rest, the one who strives with man (cf. Gen. 32:22–32 and The Book of Job). The word that man is not alone is experienced first of all as a terrifying word; the God whom we would domesticate or ignore is encountered recurrently in his wrath.

There is perhaps no concept more foreign to contemporary theology, orthodox or otherwise, than the concept of the wrath of God. The polite God of liberal theology has, like all reasonable men, learned to control his emotions. Thus there are no gargoyles in suburbia; the church looks like all the other buildings in the shopping center. Nor are there any gargoyles on the little brown church in the dell. The eschatology-theodicy of the god of orthodoxy who would destroy the world in order to save it expresses not wrath but frustration—the frustration of the law-and-order ecclesiastical managerial elite who would call their god out of his divine *apatheia* in order to justify their investment of time and reason.

The wrath of God is not the threat of end times but, as Isaiah and Amos and Jesus and Paul knew so well, it is the experience that I, here, now, am a man of unclean lips, that there is none good—no, not one—not by any definition of good and evil.

This is the God whom Job encounters. He is not the reasonable God of his friends' twaddle but the *totaliter aliter* before whom questions and reasons—even good ones like Job's—come to naught. The problems are resolved not via rational solutions; rather, they are lived with in the engagement of the whole man.

It is the service of the grotesque that it reminds us that we are not whole men—not because of gaps in our knowledge or maladjustments of the law but because we are creatures in flight from our creatureliness, men unable to die because we will not live.

With Luther, the grotesque speaks of a God more terrible than the devil. The mystery of the grotesque goes beyond the dilemmas man creates to confront man with the *mysterium tremendum* before whom his dilemmas, like Job's, grave as they may be, slip back into the shadows. Before the unrecognizable, absurd God, man can only cry out. The grotesque in the arts does infinitely more than anything else in our culture, theology included, to speak of this still real confrontation and of the human cries. To speak theologically of this confrontation and these cries is to speak of the God of wrath, the God who is the ground of our being agitated, beyond even our reasoned acquiescence to death.

This God does not come and go on invitation. As one cannot speak of his *ordo salutis,* so also one cannot speak of recovering his transcendence or expanding the consciousness of him. He is the God who happens, uninvited, unwanted.

But he happens in our midst. In the experience of the "being agitated" which the grotesque attests, there is the meeting in tension of the Unconditional in the conditional, the beyond in the here, the transcendent in the present at hand, the holy amid the common. One recognizes at once in the grotesques in art and literature that the people and the world depicted, however fantastic, are not fanciful. There is an infinite difference between Giacometti's elongated, strained figures and the ideal man created by Madison Avenue; between de Kooning's grotesque women and the centerfold of *Playboy*. The immediately evident difference is that the people of Giacometti and de Kooning are *more* real. We know them; we recognize ourselves in them and them in us. The grotesque attests not only our experience of being agitated but also confirms that this experience is ours, present and now.

To this reality of our being agitated one can compare also the artificial agitations of orthodoxy with its manipulation of blessings and curses. The grotesque attests the *viva vox,* the living voice, speaking to us from the depths of our experience and speaking in spite of our flights and our reasons. The God who is the ground of our being agitated is the God in time whose eternity is not the chronological timelessness of the cosmological or teleological arguments or the eternity of infinite primordial temporality. Rather, his eternity is the "before" of the psalmist's "Before the mountains were brought forth, or ever thou hadst formed the earth and the world, from everlasting to everlasting thou art God" (Ps. 90:2).

This "before" is that of creator before creature which is known not in a conceptual analysis of chronological time but in the harsh experience of the impossibility, the foolishness both of my flight from death and my necessary truths of reason.

Perhaps the best label for the experience of this impossibility, the experience attested in the grotesque in art and literature and in the theological confession of "uncleanness," is the term "dread" which entered our theological vocabulary from Kierkegaard. But for Kierkegaard, dread is not the last word; rather, dread is only the penultimate which creates the possibility for moving on into faith and hope.

Hope

If I make my bed in Sheol, thou art there! —Psalm 139:8

Theologically speaking, it is only out of the agony of men and the anger of God that it becomes possible to speak of hope. To those accustomed to the cheap hope of the rationalistic technological society and of rationalistic theologies, this can only sound like hyperbole at best, as another example of negativism at worst.

For the person who, like most, accepts the current middle-class *status quo* as the best of all possible worlds, the sweetest utopia that man will ever know, the hope is that these values will spread and triumph, that all men will become like the middle-class model. This results in that cheap and unfeeling irresponsibility for the world and one's fellowmen which was classically summarized in Marie Antoinette's "If there is no bread, let them eat cake" attitude. The contemporary counterpart of this is the Orphan Annie–Daddy Warbucks "pull yourself up by the bootstraps" mentality which is so pervasive in our culture. If people don't like the inner city, why don't they spend the summer at the lake or why don't they work hard so that they too can move to the suburbs? The ultimate center of the negativism which does pervade our society is precisely the middle class and its managerial elite, huddled in office and suburb, whistling in the cosmic dark, thrashing out, like Epictetus, to cut off the noses of those who cannot accept their necessary truths. As has been noted above, the theological spokesmen of this vast mass of proles offer an easy god who sanctifies success now and holds out a heavenly Linus' blanket for those who might be bothered by intimations of any eventual reckoning.

On the other hand, the apocalyptists, secular and religious, turn in bitterness from what *is* in quest of the golden age, the land without agonies and angers which is just over the horizon of the next revolution or at the end of some seventieth week of years, a telos which is eternally imminent. Whether the analysis is secular or religious, this present world is viewed as the original vale of tears, uninhabitable until that great gettin'-up morning when all men will either think right or else. In this vein, the monk leading the flagellants in Bergman's *The Seventh Seal* chastises thus:

> God has sentenced us to punishment. We shall all perish in the black death. . . . Do you know, you insensible fools, that you shall die today or tomorrow, or the next day, because all of you have been sentenced? Do you hear what I say? Do you hear the word? You have been sentenced, sentenced! [10]

According to these apocalyptists, only via conversion to their system and then only beyond the sunset of this world that is will joy become a human possibility.

In sharp contrast to this apocalyptic denigration of what is, many Biblical texts come to mind, but particularly the following passage from Luke's Gospel: "Being asked by the Pharisees when the kingdom of God was coming, he answered them, 'The Kingdom of God is not coming with signs to be observed; nor will they say, "Lo, here it is!" or "There!" for behold, the kingdom of God is in the midst of you.'" (Luke 17:20–21). Those who tell us that our only alternative to the present dystopia is an elitists' beyond, secular or religious, have never heard this word of the kingdom among us now.

The hope of this kingdom within can come only out of the agony of man and the anger of God, the agony and the anger that the grotesque attests. Anything else dissolves humanness and the present in the cheap hope of the *status quo* or the apocalypticism of perfect men in a beyond without conflict.

Over against these "hopes" we might pose this vision of life which Rilke sets before us:

> Consequently not any self-control or self-limitation for the sake of specific ends, but rather a carefree letting go of oneself. . . . Not caution but rather a wise blindness. . . . Not working to acquire silent, slowly increasing possessions, but rather a continuous squandering of all shifting values. . . . This way of being has something naïve and instinctive about it and resembles that period of the unconscious best characterized by a joyous confidence: namely the period of childhood.[11]

Rilke speaks of regaining the instincts of the child; Jesus speaks of us entering the kingdom as children; we speak of the faith of a child; Norman Brown talks of the health of the instinctual dialectic of the child. Over and again there is put before us the call to regain childlikeness. The question is, How?

From what has been said above and from what we know of children, it can be assumed that the life of isolated intellect, rationalism, is scarcely the path. Nor is the path to be found in the related call of orthodoxy which, ignoring the eternal children's question, pretends that childlikeness amounts to nothing more than shutting up and believing, i.e., accepting their collection of necessary truths. But a child knows no necessary truths.

Perhaps in what confronts us in the grotesque witness to the limits of reason and to the reality of death there may be some clue to the rebirth of childlikeness. The life of the child, with its carefree letting go, its serious play without winning, its wise blindness to things, its openness to instincts, is a life which, psychoanalytically, rests in the dialectic—not in the dualism—of the life instinct and the death instinct. Brown tells us:

> The *only* grounds for hope for humanity are in the facts
> of human childhood; and psychoanalysis is nothing with-
> out the doctrine that mankind is that species of animal
> which has the immortal project of recovering its own
> childhood; of returning to the first pre-ambivalent stage
> of the instincts which is a reality in infancy.[12]

If we can come to the point of rejecting our rationalistic flight into obeisance to death, perhaps we are on the way to regaining the childhood dialectic of the life and death instincts and thus finding release from the sick instinctual dualism of "mature" society. By speaking to us fiercely of the reality of the non-rational and of unavoidable death, the grotesque becomes a call to life and hope.

If psychoanalysis speaks of the instinctual openness of the child, theology speaks of the child as image of the acceptance of dependence. Theologically, the recovery of the life of the child begins in the experience that I am not God and in the gift of awareness that I need not be. But these are gifts given at the level of existence, not of reason. The grotesque would drive home to me my "not-godness," my dependence.

This is not the pseudo dependence of a Uriah Heep, the last resort of the con man who seeks to run life on his own terms. Rather, it is dependence like that indicated by Luther's *resignatio ad infernum,* resignation to hell, dependence in the face of a burned heaven and a quenched hell, dependence grounded in my experience, my inescapable experience, of my not-godness. It is dependence of the guts, not of the head. It is this which leads Job to say, "Though he slay me, yet will I trust in him," and to add the seldom-quoted parenthesis, "But I will maintain mine own ways before him." To come face-to-face with one's own not-godness (with which the grotesque confronts us so well) is not the end of my individuality, my personhood, but the beginning. Out of this may come the childlike dependence that makes men free, not crippled.[13]

Out of the dialectic of the life and death instincts and the awareness of my dependence, my not-godness, there can come, perhaps, the life of faith, faith like a child's. This childlike faith is not the faith that is a weaker form of knowledge, nor is it special knowledge granted with guarantees via creed or book. Bernard Martin reminds us that

> for biblical faith, knowledge—whether it is concerned
> with what have been called "truths of reason" or "truths

of fact"—is not, as it is for traditional philosophy and science, the supreme goal of human life. Against their assumption that knowledge justifies human existence . . . the Bible will insist that it is from man's living existence and experience that knowledge must obtain whatever justification it may have.[14]

Faith is that existential posture, that mode of living, which rejects all that man seeks in his quest for disposal over his future via repression and rationalism. It is the faith which begins in despair—on the other side of the truths of reason. It is the faith which grasps the absurd truth of the Christ made thief, defiler, robber, murderer, and adulterer. Also, it is the faith which affirms the Bible's impossible acclamation: "What things soever ye desire, . . . ye shall have them." [15]

Only such faith is faith in the holy; it grows out of and imitates childlikeness with its paradoxical independence within dependence beyond reason. It is faith that does not seek to become something else but rather seeks only to be more so of what it is. And it is the affirmation of life by man who is not God and who will die; thus death itself may be the rest, the sabbath of that life which is ripe.[16] Such faith is the audacity of life which accepts death; it is the audacity of life beyond reason. This faith is grounded in the experience of the holy, the experience that is attested and renewed for us, in the extremities of our rationalism, in the artists' grotesques.[17]

In Conclusion: Nothing Be Thy Name

Ernest Hemingway has a short story entitled "A Clean, Well-lighted Place" in which the main character, a waiter in a Spanish café, has the following interior monologue:

Turning off the electric light he continued the conversation with himself. . . . What did he fear? It was not fear
or dread. It was a nothing that he knew too well. It was
all a nothing and a man was nothing too. It was only that
and light was all it needed and a certain cleanness and
order. Some lived in it and never felt it but he knew it all
was nada y pues nada y nada y pues nada. Our nada who
art in nada, nada be thy name thy kingdom nada thy will
be nada in nada as it is in nada. Give us this nada our
daily nada and nada us our nada as we nada our nadas
and nada us not into nada but deliver us from nada; pues
nada. Hail nothing full of nothing, nothing is with
thee.[18]

It is not nihilism of which Hemingway speaks, nor
even in the extremities of our rationalism is it nihilism
which we need to fear. In our time the very imminent
danger is *not* that men might despair because *nihil est*,
all is meaningless. Rather, the danger rests in our many
and varied convictions that we know what is meaningful
and can and must persuade others even if, like Epictetus,
we must cut off noses in order to convince.

The ground of our knowing is our rationalism in the
service of repression, individual and societal. It is in our
knowing itself that we have bound ourselves over to
death.

The fear of the Lord is the beginning of wisdom; or,
said differently, if Nothingness is no longer the despair
of reason nor a vacuous philosophical impossibility, if
Nothingness becomes again for us, as it was for primitive
man and for Isaiah and for Pascal and for Hemingway's
waiter and for O'Connor and Buñuel and Ionesco and
the others, an experience beyond managing, then possibly we too may still live.

The voice of the grotesque in the arts and literature of our time is a living voice attesting the reality of this experience of Nothingness among us. Insofar as we share this experience, we may yet be raised up, *ex nihilo,* as the children of light.

Notes

Introduction

1. Paul Tillich, "Existentialist Aspects of Modern Art," in Carl Michalson (ed.), *Christianity and the Existentialists* (Charles Scribner's Sons, 1956), pp. 128–147.

Chapter 1. Death Is God

1. Jean Cayrol, "Night and Fog," in Robert Hughes (ed.), *Film: Book 2* (Grove Press, Inc., 1962), p. 243. *Nacht und Nebel* was, of course, the Nazi code reference to their "final solution" to the Jewish problem.

2. Compare Thomas Merton, "Chant to Be Used in Processions Around a Site with Furnaces," in Walter Lowenfels (ed.), *Where Is Vietnam? American Poets Respond* (Doubleday & Company, Inc., 1967), pp. 89–91, in which the Nazi execution camps and the American prosecution of the Indochina war are paralleled.

3. "The Winter Soldiers," *Life,* Vol. 71, No. 2 (July 9, 1971), pp. 22–26.

4. John Kerry, "The Voice of the Winter Soldier," *Playboy,*

Vol. 18, No. 8 (Aug. 1971), pp. 48–49. This is a key portion of the transcript of the testimony offered to the Senate Committee on Foreign Relations on April 22, 1971, by John Forbes Kerry, a much-decorated former naval officer, a veteran of Vietnam, and a spokesman for the Vietnam Veterans Against the War.

5. Senator Stuart Symington in *Sane World,* Feb. 14, 1968.

6. Thorstein Veblen, "Why Is Economics Not an Evolutionary Science?" in *The Place of Science in Modern Civilization and Other Essays* (New York: B. W. Huebsch, 1919), p. 73.

7. Cf. Paul Mazur, *The Standards We Raise* (Harper & Brothers, 1953), p. 32.

8. Norman O. Brown, *Life Against Death* (Vintage Books, Inc., 1959), p. 260. See also Karl Marx, *Capital,* 3 vols. (Chicago: C. H. Kerr, 1906–1909); and Émile Durkheim, *The Division of Labor in Society* (The Free Press, 1947).

9. See also Carl Skrade, "Theology and Films," in John C. Cooper and Carl Skrade (eds.), *Celluloid and Symbols* (Fortress Press, 1970), pp. 4–6.

10. Quoted by Julius Lester, "The Revolution Revisited," *Katallagete, A Journal of the Committee of Southern Churchmen,* Vol. 2, Nos. 3–4 (Winter–Spring, 1970), p. 35.

11. George Orwell, *1984.*

Chapter 2. Rationalism, Technique, and Death

1. Several of the analyses of these problems see them as inevitable and unescapable, rooted in the biological nature of man. Thus Konrad Lorenz in *On Aggression* (Harcourt, Brace & World, Inc., 1966) argues that it is the nature of the beast to be hostile, aggressive, and irrational; our current chaos is almost a fulfillment of destiny. See also Desmond Morris' *The Naked Ape* (McGraw-Hill Book Co., Inc., 1967) and Robert Ardrey's *The Territorial Imperative* (Atheneum Publishers, 1966).

2. For Alvin Toffler (*Future Shock*), Erich Fromm (*Revolution of Hope*), Andrew M. Greeley (*Come Blow Your Mind*

with Me), and Francis Schaeffer (*Escape from Reason*), the roots of our problems rest in the triumph of unreason. The cure is to be found in some form of reasonable readjustment.

But for an extensive list, the root cause is reason itself and its triumph, its practical all-pervasive application, in technology which bends man into the machineness of his machines and systems. Recent varied advocates of these views include novelists such as George Orwell (*1984*) and Aldous Huxley (*Brave New World*); social analysts such as Theodore Roszak (*The Making of a Counter-Culture*), John Cooper (*The New Mentality*), and Charles Reich (*The Greening of America*), Eugene S. Schwartz (*Overskill*), and the Freudian, Norman O. Brown (*Life Against Death*). In this same general category are philosophical-theological works such as Lev Shestov's *Athens and Jerusalem,* William Barrett's *Irrational Man,* Chad Walsh's *God at Large,* Harvey Cox's *Feast of Fools,* Sam Keen's *Apology for Wonder,* and the several works of Jacques Ellul such as *The Presence of the Kingdom, The Political Illusion,* and particularly *The Technological Society.*

3. Thomas Aquinas, *Summa Theologica* I.25.2.

4. Anders Nygren, *The Significance of the Bible for the Church* (Fortress Press, 1963), p. 3.

5. Schaeffer, *op. cit.* p. 35.

6. Cf. Rudolf Otto, *The Idea of the Holy* (London: Pelican Books, 1959), p. 73.

7. Gustave Weigel and Arthur G. Madden, *Knowledge: Its Values and Limits* (Prentice-Hall, Inc., 1961), pp. 71–72.

8. Lev Shestov, *Potestas Clavium,* tr. by Bernard Martin (Ohio University Press, 1968), pp. 10–11.

9. Ellul, *The Technological Society* (Vintage Books, Inc., 1964), p. xxv. Among Ellul's important works are *The Theological Foundations of Law* (Doubleday & Company, Inc., 1960); *The Technological Society; Propaganda: The Formation of Men's Attitudes* (The Seabury Press, Inc., 1967); and *The Political Illusion* (Alfred A. Knopf, Inc., 1967).

10. Ellul, *The Technological Society,* p. 80.

11. *Ibid.*, pp. 96 f.

12. *Ibid.*, p. 427. Similar to Ellul's cultural analysis is the later one by Roszak, *The Making of a Counter-Culture*; Roszak notes Ellul's influence on his thought. For a comparison, see Julius Lester, "The Revolution Revisited," *Katallagete*, Vol. 2, Nos. 3–4 (Winter–Spring, 1970), pp. 31–42.

13. Ellul, *The Political Illusion*, p. 220.

14. Gabriel Vahanian, "Theology, Politics and the Christian Faith," *Katallagete*, Vol. 2, Nos. 3–4 (Winter–Spring, 1970), pp. 19 f.

15. Ellul, *The Presence of the Kingdom* (The Seabury Press, Inc., 1967), p. 28.

16. Christopher Lasch, "The Social Thought of Jacques Ellul," *Katallagete*, Vol. 2, Nos. 3–4 (Winter–Spring, 1970), pp. 27 ff. Lasch implies a corrective in the direction of socialism. I feel we must push beyond this suggestion also and seek after the psychological-theological roots of both technique and waste which happens in capitalism, communism, *and* socialism.

17. *Ibid.*

18. *Ibid.*, p. 30.

19. I feel that one cannot overemphasize the significance of Freud or his excellent American interpreter, Norman O. Brown. Brown's two basic works, *Life Against Death* and *Love's Body*, need increased theological attention. Peter Homans' *Theology After Freud* is a most perceptive and welcome attempt to break new ground. The works of both Brown and Homans are rich in bibliographical suggestions. See also R. D. Laing's works, especially *The Divided Self* (Penguin Books, Inc., 1965).

20. Norman O. Brown, *Life Against Death*, pp. 79–81.

21. See Richard Rubinstein, *After Auschwitz* (The Bobbs-Merrill Company, Inc., 1966).

22. Brown, *Life Against Death*, pp. 105 f.

23. Cf. Vine Deloria, Jr., *Custer Died for Your Sins: An Indian Manifesto* (The Macmillan Company, 1969), pp. 122 f.

24. Brown, *Life Against Death*, in the section entitled "Filthy

Lucre" (pp. 234–304) in tightly reasoned and meticulous arguments analyzes the anality and death orientation of the money complex in contemporary culture. The reader is directed to this work for the bases of the conclusions I have stated here.

25. Brown, *Life Against Death*, pp. 236 ff. However, unlike Marx, Brown points out that the villain is not capitalism or any external system, but rather "something in the human psyche which commits man to non-enjoyment."

26. Brown, *Life Against Death*, pp. 75–133 especially.

27. *Ibid.*, p. 104.

28. *Ibid.*

29. *Ibid.*, p. 116.

30. Shestov, *Athens and Jerusalem*, tr. by Bernard Martin (Simon & Schuster, Inc., 1968), p. 69; see also Peter Damian's understanding of original sin.

31. *Ibid.*, p. 32. This is Bernard Martin's summary of Shestov's evaluation of speculative philosophy in Martin's excellent introduction to his translation of *Athens and Jerusalem*.

Chapter 3. Beyond Rationalism

1. This type of description of God, so typical of orthodox Christianity, is scarcely distinguishable from Plato's description of God in *The Republic*.

2. Plato, *Theaetetus*, 196D.

3. Luther, Sermon on Exodus, ch. 20: "Yea, for the world it seemeth as though God were a mere silly yawner, with mouth ever agape, or a cuckold, who lets another lie with his wife and feigneth that he sees it not.

"But He assaileth a man, and hath *such a delight* therein that He is of His jealousy and wrath impelled to *consume* the wicked.

"Then shall we learn how that God is a consuming fire. . . . Wilt thou sin? Then will He *devour thee up.* . . . For God is a fire that consumeth, devoureth, rageth, verily He is your undoing, as fire consumeth a house and maketh it dust and ashes."

4. Luther, *Commentary on the Epistle to the Galatians* (Zondervan Publishing House, 1939).

5. Luther, *Commentary on Romans* (Zondervan Publishing House, 1954).

6. F. M. Dostoevsky, *Notes from the Underground* (E. P. Dutton & Co., Inc., 1960).

7. Ludwig Wittgenstein, *Philosophical Investigations,* ed. by George Pitcher (Doubleday & Company, Inc., Anchor Book, 1966).

8. Albert Camus, *The Myth of Sisyphus and Other Essays* (Alfred A. Knopf, Inc., 1955), p. 19.

9. In this allusion, I am assuming the debatable authenticity of Amos' doxologies.

10. Rudolf Otto, *The Idea of the Holy,* p. 74.

11. *Ibid.,* p. 42.

12. *Ibid.,* p. 124.

13. Augustine, *Confessions* 2.9.1.

14. Otto, *op. cit.,* p. 24.

15. *Ibid.,* pp. 112 f.

16. *Ibid., passim;* especially pp. 69 ff., 149–152.

17. Shestov, *Athens and Jerusalem,* pp. 68–69.

18. I am particularly indebted to Arthur Clayborough's study *The Grotesque in English Literature* (Oxford: Clarendon Press, 1965), for the information on the historical development of the category of the grotesque. This book and that by Wolfgang Kayser, *The Grotesque in Art and Literature* (Peter Smith, 1968), are the studies of the grotesque which I have found most valuable. Also of interest in the literature on the grotesque are the following: Braun, Fuchs, Hausner, Lehmden, *Die Wiener Schule des phantastischen Realismus* (Berlin: Galerie Sydow, 1965); T. T. Wildridge, *The Grotesque in Church Art* (London: W. Andrews, 1899); Lester B. Bridham, *Gargoyles, Chimeras and the Grotesque in French Gothic Sculpture* (Anchor Book Publishing Company, 1930); William Van O'Connor, *The Grotesque: An American Genre* (South-

ern Illinois University Press, 1962); Luigi Ferrante, *Teatro Italiano Grottesco* (Bologna: Cappelli, 1964); Théophile Gautier, *Les Grotesques* (Paris: E. Fasquelle, 1913); Wolfgang Promies, *Die Bürger und der Narr, oder Das Risiko der Phantasie* (Munich: Hauser, 1966); G. L. Van Roosbrock, *Grotesques* (New York: Living Art, 1929); Mary Cass Canfield, *Grotesques and Other Reflections* (Harper & Brothers, 1927); Hector Berlioz, *Les Grotesques de la musique* (Paris: Librairie Nouvelle, 1859); Gerhardus van der Leeuw, *Sacred and Profane Beauty* (Holt, Rinehart & Winston, Inc., 1963); Ulrich Conrads and Hans G. Sperlich, *The Architecture of Fantasy* (Frederick A. Praeger, Inc., 1960); *Das Groteske im modernen Drama: Sinn oder Unsinn* (Basel: Basilius Presse, 1962); Arnold Heidsieck, *Das Groteske und das Absurde im modernen Drama* (Stuttgart: Kohlhammer, 1969); Jurgis Baltrusaitis, *Aberrations, quatre essais sur la légende des formes* (Paris: O. Perrin, 1957); Howard Daniel, *Devils, Monsters and Nightmares: An Introduction to the Grotesque and Fantastic in Art* (London: Abelard-Schuman, 1964); Deutsche Gesellschaft für bildende Kunst, *Labyrinthe: Phantastische Kunst vom 16 Jahrhundert bis zum Gegenwart* (Berlin: Eberhard Rotors, 1966); René de Solier, *L'Art fantastique* (Paris: J.-J. Pauvert, 1961); Malcolm Anstett Griffith, "The Grotesque in American Fiction" (unpublished Ph.D. thesis, Ohio State University, 1966); Ernst Fuchs, *Architectura Coelestis* (Salzburg: Residenz Verlag, 1966); Michael M. Prechtel, *Ars Phantastica: Deutsche Kunst des magischen Realismus, phantastischen Realismus, und Surrealismus seit 1945* (Nuremberg: Albrecht Gesellschaft, 1967); Robert M. Doty, *Human Concern/Personal Torment: The Grotesque in American Art* (Frederick A. Praeger, Inc., 1969); Wilhelm Michel, *Das Teufelische und Groteske in der Kunst* (Munich: R. Piper, 1919); Alfred H. Barr (ed.), *Fantastic Art, Dada and Surrealism* (Museum of Modern Art, 1936); Herbert Read, *Art and Alienation* (Horizon Press, 1967); George Selz, *New Images of Man* (Museum of Modern Art, 1959); Paul Fierens, *Le Fantastique dans l'art flammand* (Brussels: Éditions du Circle d'Art, 1947); Philip Thomson, *The Grotesque* (London: Methuen and Co., Ltd., 1972).

19. Clayborough, *op. cit.*, p. 2; see also Kayser, *op. cit.*, Ch. I.

20. This style was not limited to Rome at this time, but probably came into Rome under influences from Asia Minor. See Clayborough's quotation from *De Architectura* by Marcus Vitruvius Pallio; Clayborough, *op. cit.*, pp. 19–20.

21. Clayborough, *op. cit.*, p. 16. "Incongruity with the real and normal" demands, of course, the further questions as to what is real and normal and who is to decide.

22. Clayborough, *op. cit.*, p. 22.

23. Actually, it seems to me that the fourth approach suggested by Clayborough necessarily involves elements of the first and second. The first approach, in and of itself, is difficult because of the inaccessibility of the *Schaffenvorgang;* also, the artist himself often seems unclear as to his motivations and intentions. The second approach is of limited value by itself because the response of the audience involves so many contingencies and varies so widely.

Chapter 4. The Grotesque in Fiction: Flannery O'Connor

1. Flannery O'Connor's basic works are collected in the following: *Flannery O'Connor: The Complete Stories* (Farrar, Straus & Giroux, Inc., 1971); Sally and Robert Fitzgerald (eds.), *Mystery and Manners: Occasional Prose* (Farrar, Straus & Giroux, Inc., 1957). Her novels are *The Violent Bear It Away* (1960) and *Wise Blood* (1952), published by Farrar, Straus & Giroux, Inc. There have been many fine essays and some book-length studies of Miss O'Connor and her craft. However, a definitive study has not yet arrived, nor is it being attempted here. For a good bibliography of studies of O'Connor, see Josephine Hendin, *The World of Flannery O'Connor* (Indiana University Press, 1970).

2. Flannery O'Connor, "Some Aspects of the Grotesque in

Southern Fiction," in Sally and Robert Fitzgerald (eds.), *Mystery and Manners* (The Noonday Press, 1969), p. 41.

3. *Ibid.*, pp. 42 f.

4. Preston M. Browning, Jr., "Flannery O'Connor and the Grotesque Recovery of the Holy," in Nathan Scott (ed.), *Adversity and Grace* (The University of Chicago Press, 1968), pp. 159–160.

5. O'Connor, "Some Aspects of the Grotesque in Southern Fiction," *loc. cit.*, p. 40.

6. *Ibid.*, p. 43.

7. Flannery O'Connor, *Everything That Rises Must Converge* (Farrar, Straus & Giroux, Inc., 1965), p. xx. From a personal letter to Robert Fitzgerald.

8. It has been suggested frequently that O'Connor was not opposed to Pentecostal movements, that she focused her wrath more on liberalism than on Pentecostalism or orthodox Christianity. This is hardly the case. Her distinctions were not between Pentecostalism, liberalism, or traditional religion but rather quite simply between a religion that a man could manipulate for his own reasonable ends, here and hereafter, and a religion of the unappeasable, unmanageable *totaliter aliter* to whom all, irrevocably, belong. Onnie Jay Holy (Hoover Shoates) of *Wise Blood* does not differ essentially from Mrs. Hopewell and Mrs. Freeman of "Good Country People," plainly orthodox types. Compare also the orthodox prattle about the temple of the Holy Ghost (talk which most women who were brought up in Catholic schools remember well) in the story by that name.

9. Browning, "Flannery O'Connor and the Grotesque Recovery of the Holy," in Scott (ed.), *op. cit.*, p. 143.

10. *Ibid.*, p. 146.

11. Otto, *op. cit.*, p. 117.

12. *Ibid.*, p. 115. Otto offers this quote, but in caution before this boldness adds quickly that it is "an assumption which would be in fact a dangerous and erroneous one; for no distinction of the non-rational and the rational aspects of God

would imply that the latter is less essential than the former."

13. This phrase, "Everything that rises must converge," is the title of another of O'Connor's short stories and, of course, a much-quoted line from Teilhard de Chardin.

Chapter 5. The Grotesque in Film:
Buñuel and Fellini

1. Ado Kyrou, *Luis Buñuel: An Introduction* (Simon & Schuster, Inc., 1963), p. 19.

2. *Ibid.*, p. 18.

3. John R. Taylor, *Cinema Eye, Cinema Ear: Some Key Film-Makers of the Sixties* (Hill & Wang, 1967), p. 87.

4. Luis Buñuel, *Three Screenplays* (The Viking Press, Inc., 1969).

5. Taylor, *op. cit.*, p. 110.

6. Buñuel quoted in Taylor, *op. cit.*, p. 96.

7. Kyrou, *op. cit.*, p. 89.

8. *Ibid.*, pp. 121–125. From a 1961 interview of Buñuel by Elena Poniatowski.

9. Kyrou, *op. cit.*, pp. 124 and 120 respectively; from interviews with Buñuel.

10. Taylor, *op. cit.*, pp. 43–44.

11. Federico Fellini, *Fellini's Satyricon* (Ballantine Books, Inc., 1970), pp. 29 f.

12. See also Harvey Cox, "The Purpose of the Grotesque in Fellini's Films," in Cooper and Skrade (eds.), *Celluloid and Symbols*, pp. 89–106.

13. *Ibid.*, pp. 3–27.

14. Ingmar Bergman, *Four Screenplays of Ingmar Bergman* (Simon & Schuster, Inc., 1960), p. 109.

15. *Ibid.*, p. 163.

16. A good basic, if anecdotal, history of the horror film is Carlos Clarens, *An Illustrated History of the Horror Film* (G. P. Putnam's Sons, Inc., Capricorn Books, 1967).

Chapter 6. The Grotesque in Other Arts:
Picasso and Ionesco

1. One of the most distinctive happenings in the world of art in the past century has been this surge of interest in primitives, children's art, and the art of the insane.

2. Kayser, *op. cit.*, p. 175.

3. Alfred Kubin, *Alfred Kubin's Autobiography, The Other Side* (George Wittenborn, Inc., 1970).

4. Otto, *op. cit.*, p. 123.

5. George Grosz, *A Big No and a Little Yes* (The Dial Press, Inc., 1946), p. 163.

6. There is, of course, a very extensive body of primary and secondary literature concerning surrealism. Works that I have found helpful include André Breton, *Manifestoes of Surrealism* (University of Michigan Press, 1969); Anna E. Balakian, *Literary Origins of Surrealism* (New York University Press, 1966); J. H. Matthews, *An Introduction to Surrealism* (Pennsylvania State University Press, 1965); Maurice Nadeau, *The History of Surrealism* (The Macmillan Company, 1965); Yves Duplessis, *Surrealism* (Walker & Company, 1962).

7. Kayser, *op. cit.*, p. 188.

8. O. F. Beer, "Surrealismus und Psychoanalyse," *Plan*, Vol. V (1947), pp. 329–330.

9. Duplessis, *op. cit.*, p. 26. "Surrealism," he states, "is essentially an implied and intuitive criticism of conventional thought patterns, a force that takes a fact, or a collection of facts, from what is considered a normal context, and throws it into a dazzling display of unexpected and super-real juxtapositions. By mixing reality and fantasy outside the limits of everyday realism and reasoned logic, it . . . lends to its surroundings a grotesque newness."

10. *Ibid.*, p. 133.

11. A. H. Barr, *Picasso: Fifty Years of His Art* (Museum of Modern Art, 1946), p. 200.

12. In the analysis that follows I am particularly indebted to Otto J. Brendel's essay "Classic and Non-Classic Elements in Picasso's Guernica," in Whitney J. Oates (ed.), *From Sophocles to Picasso* (Indiana University Press, 1962), pp. 121–159, and to Barr, *op. cit.*

13. See Brendel, *loc. cit.*, pp. 135–136; also D. E. Schneider, "The Painting of Pablo Picasso: A Psychoanalytical Study," *College Art Journal* VII (1947–48), pp. 86 ff.

14. Quoted by Barr, *op. cit.*, p. 273.

15. See Brendel, *loc. cit.*, pp. 144–145; Paul Tillich, "Existentialist Aspects of Modern Art," in Michalson, *op. cit.*, pp. 144 ff.

16. Paul Tillich, "A Prefatory Note," in Peter Selz, *New Images of Men*, p. 10.

17. Otto, *op. cit.*, p. 84.

18. There are interesting parallels between the work of Fellini as discussed above and that of John Cage: both express the experience of the *mysterium fascinans.*

19. See also Kayser, *op. cit.*, pp. 11–12.

20. Eugène Ionesco, "Expérience du theatre," *Nouvelle Revue Française*, Paris, Feb. 1, 1958, p. 253.

21. E. Ionesco, "La Tragédie du language," *Spectacles*, Paris, No. 2, July, 1958. Quoted by Martin Esslin, *The Theatre of the Absurd* (Doubleday & Company, Inc., Anchor Book, 1961), p. 84.

22. Esslin, *op. cit.*, pp. 290–291.

Chapter 7. Hope Beyond Reason

1. Compare Lev Shestov, *Athens and Jerusalem*, p. 436, concerning "idle questions": "He who asks, what times is it? or what is the density of mercury? needs, indeed, to be given a determinate answer, and this suffices for him. But he who asks if God is just or the soul immortal wants something quite other; and clear and distinct answers make him furious or plunge him into despair. How is one to make people under-

stand this? How is one to explain to them that somewhere, beyond a certain limit, the human soul is so completely transformed that the very 'mechanism' of thought becomes something quite other, or, to put it better, there is no longer any place for mechanism in this thought."

2. Sam Keen, "Man and Myth: A Conversation with Joseph Campbell," *Psychology Today*, Vol. 5, No. 2 (July 1971), p. 95.

3. As is obvious to anyone acquainted with Norman Brown's work, I am deeply indebted to him for this discussion. See especially *Life Against Death*, Ch. 8. Brown, pp. 100–101, notes: "If death is a part of life, there is a peculiar morbidity in the human attitude toward death—a morbidity which Freud recognized but did not connect with his theory of the death instinct. . . . It is not the consciousness of death but the flight from death that distinguishes men from animals. . . . If death is a part of life, man represses his own death just as he represses his own life."

4. See Herbert Braun, *Gesammelte Studien zum Neuen Testament und seinem Umwelt* (Tübingen: J. C. B. Mohr, 1962).

5. Rudolf Bultmann, "The Idea of God and Modern Man," in Robert Funk *et al.* (eds.), *Translating Theology Into the Modern Age* (Harper & Row, Publishers, Inc., 1965), pp. 83–95, especially pp. 91–95.

6. Braun, *op. cit.*, p. 341.

7. Bultmann, *loc. cit.*, p. 94.

8. Cf. Otto, *op. cit., passim.*

9. Otto, *op. cit.*, p. 114. Concerning Luther's experience of this God, Otto says: "That before which his soul quails again and again in awe is not merely the stern Judge demanding righteousness . . . but rather at the same time God in his 'unrevealedness,' in the aweful majesty of His very Godhead; He before whom trembles not simply the transgressor of the law, but the creature, as such, in his 'uncovered' creaturehood."

10. Bergman, *op. cit.*, p. 124.

11. Rilke, *Über Kunst,* quoted in Brown, *op. cit.,* p. 237.

12. Brown, *op. cit.,* p. 84.

13. Thus Bernard Martin in his introduction to Shestov's *Athens and Jerusalem,* p. 31, notes: "Having created man, God blessed him, gave him dominion over all the universe and bestowed upon him the essentially divine and most precious of all gifts, freedom. Man is not, unless he renounces his primordial freedom (as all men, in fact, tend to do in their obsession with obtaining rational explanation and scientific knowledge), under the power of universal and necessary causal laws or unalterable empirical facts."

14. *Ibid.*

15. *Ibid.,* p. 68. Shestov tells us, "In Scripture . . . faith . . . is that dimension of thought where truth abandons itself fearlessly and joyously to the entire disposition of the Creator: 'Thy will be done!' The will of Him who, on his side, fearlessly and with sovereign power returns to the believer his lost power: . . . 'What things soever ye desire . . . ye shall have them.' " It is here that there begins for fallen man the region, forever condemned by reason, of the miraculous and of the fantastic.

16. Brown, *op. cit.,* p. 93, states: "But if repression were overcome and man could enjoy the life proper to his species, the regressive fixation to the past would dissolve; the restless quest for novelty would be reabsorbed into the desire for pleasurable repetition; the desire to Become would be reabsorbed into the desire to Be."

17. See also Otto, *op. cit.,* pp. 120–121.

18. Ernest Hemingway, "A Clean, Well-lighted Place," *The Hemingway Reader* (Charles Scribner's Sons, 1953), p. 421. I am indebted to William Barrett, *Irrational Man* (Doubleday & Company, Inc., Anchor Book, 1958), pp. 283–294, for the suggestion of this passage and its significance.